A REVISION OF
DEMAND THEORY

A REVISION OF DEMAND THEORY

BY

J. R. HICKS

DRUMMOND PROFESSOR OF POLITICAL ECONOMY
IN THE UNIVERSITY OF OXFORD

OXFORD
AT THE CLARENDON PRESS

Oxford University Press, Ely House, London W.1

GLASGOW NEW YORK TORONTO MELBOURNE WELLINGTON
CAPE TOWN SALISBURY IBADAN NAIROBI LUSAKA ADDIS ABABA
BOMBAY CALCUTTA MADRAS KARACHI LAHORE DACCA
KUALA LUMPUR SINGAPORE HONG KONG TOKYO

FIRST PUBLISHED 1956

REPRINTED LITHOGRAPHICALLY IN GREAT BRITAIN
AT THE UNIVERSITY PRESS, OXFORD
FROM CORRECTED SHEETS OF THE FIRST EDITION
1959, 1965, 1969

PREFACE

THE demand theory which I am 'revising' in this book is that of the first three chapters of my *Value and Capital*; I have felt that this theory does need some reconsideration, in the light of the work which has been done during the seventeen years which have elapsed since it was first published. I can nevertheless maintain that the original version stands up to the revision pretty well. I do not now think that the methodology was quite as it should have been; some of the treatment was too elliptic, and some difficulties, which deserved more serious attention, were brushed aside; most important of all, some opportunities were missed. I nevertheless expect that there will be some readers who will continue to prefer the 1939 version. Those who rely upon mathematical methods will not get much from the present approach which they could not get from the mathematical appendix to *Value and Capital*; but those to whom those methods are uncongenial, and those who feel that the use of calculus in economic analysis requires justification (such as it commonly receives in statistics), are more likely to find that the present version is an improvement.

I do not wish to present this volume as a mere report on my own further thinking. It has been profoundly influenced by others. Such time as I could devote to these matters during the war years was occupied in working out the consequences of a most fruitful suggestion by the late Alexander Henderson—a suggestion which led to my present theory of consumer's surplus (Chapters X and XVIII of this book). It was not until 1946 that I came under wider influences: Samuelson, Lange, Mosak, and René Roy, to name only those who most affected me in this field at that time. Perhaps I may be allowed to recall an occasion in the autumn of 1946, at Harvard, when I was called upon to expound my work on consumer's surplus to a most select audience of five or six (which included Samuelson). It was then that Samuelson showed me how I could get most of my results, much more simply and neatly, in terms of his 'Σpq's'; though on reflection I already felt called upon to reply that there are some purposes for which a marginal analysis remains essential—especially for the derivation of those properties which depend upon the use of linear approximations to the marginal curves. In that discussion the seed of this book was already sown. But as it has grown in my mind, it has been subjected to other influences: first of all that of Samuelson's book (which did not appear until 1947), then of those who may perhaps be called his followers, among whom Arrow, Little, and Houthakker must be especially mentioned. It was Houthakker's 1950 article, with its demonstration that transitivity is the 'logical' counterpart of integrability, which (from my point of view) supplied the missing link and tied the whole of the 'logical' theory together. All this I owe to Samuelson and the Samuelsonians, though I can hardly count myself of their number, since I retain a considerable scepticism about the 'Revealed Preference' approach. It is a long-standing trouble of demand theory that it is always tempting us to overplay our hand. I have here attempted to show that we can interpret the theory in an extremely modest manner, and still have a theory which will do everything for us that we need ask of it.

In the autumn of 1951 I gave a course of public lectures at the London School of Economics, on 'Demand and Welfare'; in one of these lectures I gave a sketch of what was to become the central part of this book. Much of the book was written soon after that date, but other occupations have caused its completion to be much delayed. Even now, it has been necessary to postpone what I have to say on the 'Welfare' side to another occasion. Here I would merely say that my neglect of the 'Welfare' side in this book does not mean that I have not attended to it; I hope in fact to have a good deal to say about it later on.

Though I have made use of the works of the writers whom I have mentioned, I am very well aware that there are others, from whom I could have learned something (perhaps much) but whose work I have been unable to absorb. Some of these (such as Wold[1] and Stone[2]) have seemed to me to be mainly concerned with the statistical application of the theory, rather than with the theory itself; and that is a matter which I have

---

[1] H. Wold (with L. Juréen), *Demand Analysis*.
[2] J. R. N. Stone, *The Role of Measurement in Economics*.

felt obliged to regard as being outside my field. But there are no doubt others for whom I cannot even plead this excuse. For them I would only say that the time came when my own construction had to be allowed to take charge: as I learned to my cost, even quite small alterations (as for instance in terminology) involved the most extensive rewriting. Once the thing had seriously started its own logic compelled me to continue writing it in its own way.

Thus the acknowledgements which I have to make are mainly to those writers whom I have cited above, and to a few others whose works I cite in the course of the book. But my acknowledgements do not merely extend to their published writings; I have had the advantage of personal discussion with (I think) all of the contemporary writers to whom I refer. Even Mr. Ichimura, who plays a considerable part in my Chapter XVII, and who was for long an exception, dropped in on me from Japan at a most convenient moment. To all of them I offer my thanks: as also to Mr. Faaland, of Nuffield College, who read the whole manuscript in a nearly finished form, and made a number of most useful suggestions, some of which (even then) I was able to adopt.

J. R. H.

Oxford
September 1955

Postscript to Preface (June 1958)

I have taken advantage of this reprinting to make some small alterations to two passages (on pp. 40 and 71) which have been subject to particular criticism; and to add a Note at the end of the book justifying what I have done.

CONTENTS

PART I

FOUNDATIONS

I

THE ECONOMETRIC APPROACH

1. By the Theory of Demand, as I shall use the term in this book, I mean nothing else but the conventional theory of 'utility' and consumers' choice, which finds a place, in some form or other, in all modern textbooks of economics. I am by no means concerned to assert that this approach is the only possible approach to the economics of consumption; it may well be that at the next round other approaches will have more to offer. But, even while keeping within the bounds of the traditional theory, I still feel that I have something to say. Though by now nearly all the propositions which seem to belong to the theory are well known to mathematical economists, they are not so well known to non-mathematicians. I believe that a point has now been reached when the *whole* theory can be set out in relatively simple terms, terms in which the economic significance of what is being done can be made much more readily apparent. As it is, the foundations of the theory are still to some extent a matter of controversy; the fuller statement which is now possible should clear up some of these methodological controversies also. A fuller appreciation of what can be achieved in certain directions helps one to understand the limitations, as well as the strength, of the general approach.

2. During the three-quarter century of its existence, demand theory has passed through four recognizable stages. The culmination of the first stage was in Marshall's *Principles* (1890). Behind Marshall we do not need to go, for little which was written on this subject before Marshall has anything which will help us here. Marshall, on the other hand, remains classic; almost everything which Marshall says in his Book III retains its validity and requires, in some form or other, to be kept. And the things which Marshall said were the really important things. Though the Marshallian core is itself bound to look rather different when the newer appurtenances have been added to it than it did when it stood in isolation, we should recognize that the core is still there. We have come, in some ways, to talk a different language; but the substance of what we have to say, over a central part of the field, is the same as what Marshall said.

From this point of view, the work of Marshall's successors may be regarded as the extension of his technique to cover more complicated problems than those with which he attempted to deal; this, in the end, was precisely what was to come of their efforts. But in the meantime it often appeared that there was a more substantial change in approach. If we take the case of Pareto, whose *Manuel* (1906 in its original Italian version) must mark our second stage, his essential contribution was to *pose* the wider problems. While Marshall's theory was organized so as to meet the needs of his partial equilibrium technique (so that he concentrated attention on the demand for a single commodity in terms of the rest), Pareto's was oriented in the direction of general equilibrium, the *set* of quantities (of the various commodities demanded) depending on the *set* of prices. Pareto accordingly thought of Marshall's theory as being no more than a special case of his own—as being derivable from his own theory by letting only one price vary, instead of many prices. But Pareto did not in fact do as much with the wider problem as Marshall had done with the narrower. His theory was less operative than Marshall's; though he added to our understanding of the working of the price-system, he did not provide a theory which was easily capable of being applied. The third stage of development, which may be taken to run from the celebrated articles of Johnson[1] and Slutsky[2] up to my own *Value and Capital* (1939), accordingly includes a number of attempts to improve upon Pareto in this particular respect.

It may be claimed that some progress was made by the writers of this group towards making the Pareto theory more usable,

[1] W. E. Johnson, 'The Pure Theory of Utility Curves' (*Econ. Jour.* 1913).
[2] E. Slutsky, 'Sulla teoria del bilancio del consumatore' (*Giornale degli Economisti*, 1915).

and at the same time towards weaving the Marshallian and Paretian threads together. Though the terminology, and the diagrammatic apparatus, remained Paretian, the substance of the theory drew steadily closer to Marshall. As time went on, mere terminological differences were bound to decline in importance.

From some points of view, and they are important points of view, that is all that had happened by the end of the third stage. We were back with Marshall, having reinterpreted him a little in order to make his theory applicable to more complicated problems than those with which he wanted to deal. It looked, and often felt, very like the end of the story.

3. But it was not the end of the story, because of a new development, which already affected the work done in the nineteen-thirties, and which separates that work, not merely from Marshall, but from Pareto also. Something had happened which the newer writers had to take into account, but which the older writers had not had to take into account. This new development was the rise of Econometrics.

It is certainly not the case that the econometric reference of the new theories was at first very explicit. It is not at all explicit in *Value and Capital*; it could hardly have been made so, since the general course of the argument of that book was to proceed far away from any econometric application. But it is true that at crucial points the argument was put in a form which was influenced by what the econometrists had been doing, and by the problems which had come up in their work. I think I may justly conclude that the potential econometric reference was one of the reasons why the book was as well received as it was. For whatever we think of the results that the econometrists have attained, there can be no doubt that econometrics is now a major form of economic research; a theory which can be used by econometrists is to that extent a better theory than one which cannot. The theory which had been reached at the end of the third stage (roughly speaking, that which is expressed in the first three chapters of *Value and Capital*) did at least begin to have this particular merit.

But it was a defect—a serious defect—that the econometric reference was not made more explicit. The ideal theory of demand, for econometric purposes, is still not precisely that which had been reached at the point just described. Further important developments lay ahead. The beginning (but perhaps not the end) of the fourth stage in our story must be associated with Samuelson's *Foundations of Economic Analysis* (1947). In Samuelson the whole form of the theory is allowed to be dictated by the reference to econometrics. Great and beautiful simplifications follow. But I am not convinced that even in Samuelson the econometric reference is quite as it should be, so that the present work, deeply influenced by Samuelson as it is, will not follow him at all exactly. In technique we shall keep quite close to him, but our methodology will be more explicitly econometric even than his.

4. That the logical structure of the theory is improved by this econometric reference is a thing which I believe I shall be able to demonstrate; but it may well be maintained that in pursuing this course we are making too much of the application to econometrics, and are setting the whole theory on too narrow a base. Let us see what it is that we are in danger of leaving out. What, in fact, are the other things which the theory of demand is expected to do, in addition to making itself useful to econometrists? In order to answer this question, it will be well to look for a moment at the position before the econometric invasion, which means, in accordance with what has been said above, looking particularly at the state of the theory in its Marshallian phase.

If one had asked, at the time of Marshall, what demand theory was for, two answers could I think have been given, leading to two distinct purposes. One, which we may here call the Plain Economic purpose, was related to the ordinary job of the economist, the making of good guesses about the consequences of economic events and economic policies. The other, which we will here call the Welfare purpose, is the application to Welfare Economics. These two purposes raise quite different issues, and must be considered separately.

5. Even apart from demand theory, the economist has at his disposal for the purpose of prognostication (1) certain identical relations between economic magnitudes—'If you use more steel for armaments, you will have less for other purposes, unless you make more steel or import more steel', (2) technological relations of what may broadly be called an engineering character, about the output which can be got from available plant, and the labour and materials needed to produce it. But these relations, though even by themselves they carry us a surprisingly long way (as the 'input-output' analysis of Professor Leontief and his collaborators is showing us today in a new manner) do not by themselves get us as far as we can reasonably hope to get. We need rules which will tell us something about the behaviour, not of material equipment, but of human beings. So far as man the producer (or at least the entrepreneur) is concerned, it has commonly been thought that adequate rules could be got from the principle of maximizing money gain—the economic man. (Whether this principle is adequate even in the case of the entrepreneur is a thing about which modern economists feel increasingly doubtful.) In the case of the consumer such an assumption is clearly insufficient, but it was natural to approach the behaviour of the consumer in something like the same way, and to look about for something which he might be considered to maximize. Thus we got the Utility theory, the consequences of which were set out by Marshall in classic form.

Now though Plain Economics existed long before econometrics, and is practised by many people who would not call themselves econometrists, it is not clear that the requirements of plain economics and of econometrics are really any different. Plain economics is solely concerned with the objective consequences of economic events. The human individual only comes into plain economics as an entity which reacts in certain ways to certain stimuli; all that the Plain Economist needs to be interested in are the laws of his reactions. Now it is precisely these laws which the econometrist is endeavouring to study, by methods which are empirical as well as theoretical. In so far as the econometrist has any success in using theory to increase our empirical knowledge of human behaviour, the plain economist must be helped in his understanding of economic processes, and his ability to forecast must be improved. The relation between the two purposes is too close for it to be sensible to have a different theory for each purpose; if the new theory is more suitable than the old for the purposes of the econometrist, it can hardly fail to be at least as suitable as the old for the purposes of the plain economist.

The plain economist should therefore be easily pacified; it is the other purpose, the welfare purpose, which causes the trouble.

6. If one starts from a theory of demand like that of Marshall and his contemporaries, it is exceedingly natural to look for a welfare application. If the general aim of the economic system is the satisfaction of consumers' wants, and if the satisfaction of individual wants is to be conceived of as a maximizing of Utility, cannot the aim of the system be itself conceived of as a maximizing of utility, Universal Utility as Edgeworth[1] called it? If this could be done, and some measure of universal utility could be found, the economist's function could be widened out, from the understanding of cause and effect to the judgement of the effects—whether, from the point of view of want-satisfaction they are to be judged as successful or unsuccessful, good or bad. Economists have always felt that such judgement or assessment was in some way a part of their business. Demand theory, in its Marshallian form, appeared to offer a strikingly simple and powerful way of making such judgements. The method which resulted from this application enabled Marshall himself to arrive at conclusions of startling originality (as in his theory of Increasing Returns); and it was elaborated in the great work of Professor Pigou which has given a name (not, perhaps, a very fortunate name) to this branch of economics.

It must be admitted—and indeed emphasized—that the econometric theory of demand provides no such easy and natural transition to welfare economics as the Marshallian theory appeared to give us. The econometric theory of demand does study human beings, but only as entities having certain patterns of market behaviour; it makes no claim, no pretence, to be able to see inside their heads. But welfare economics has a strong tendency to go farther—if we like, to aim higher. There is therefore a chasm which has to be passed, a bridge which needs to be built.

I do not believe that it is impossible to build such a bridge, and I intend (in a later work) to make as precise a statement as I can of the way in which I would now endeavour to built it. But

---

[1] *Mathematical Psychics*, pp. 15–16.

it seems to me to be of the first importance to realize that there is a problem here—a very great problem, which cannot be solved without much care and circumspection. Experience has shown that the easy passage, which the older theory appeared to offer, was highly treacherous. Conclusions of great importance were reached by that route, conclusions which do undoubtedly possess a certain kind of validity; but the arguments by which the conclusions were supported were less convincing than the conclusions themselves, so that the kind of validity which was to be attributed to the conclusions remained rather uncertain. I now believe that these conclusions can be brought into a harmonious relation with the econometric approach to non-welfare problems. If this can be done, it must clarify our ideas about validity; though it will never succeed in making the conclusions uncontroversial, it should narrow the range of controversy. If anything of this proves to be true, there will be no need to apologize for the inability of our approach to give an easy access to welfare economics. It is better that we should be challenged to set our welfare economics on a firm basis than that we should be led to suppose that there is no problem to be solved.

7. With these general remarks, I leave the discussion of applications, and turn to the theory itself. But I shall not commence my own formulation of it until we reach Chapter III. For there is a dragon waiting at the door who must first be cleared out of the way. It is the old crux of the measurability of utility.

II

THE MEASURABILITY OF UTILITY

1. The assumption that utility is not measurable—that it is an ordinal, not a cardinal, concept—appears on the surface to be a hall-mark of those theories which descend from Pareto, as against those which descend from Marshall. It thus appears to be a matter of taste, or of philosophical preconception. But it is more fundamental, so far as modern work is concerned, to regard the ordinal hypothesis as a mark of the econometric approach. The precise connexion between it and the econometric approach can perhaps be made clear in the following way.[1]

It is certainly not the case that the econometrist is obliged to *believe* that utility is purely ordinal. He does not claim to be able to prove a universal negative. If he has some independent reason for believing in the possibility of a cardinal measure, there is nothing in the nature of the econometric problem which can shake his belief. If he sees some advantage, in some other field of research (perhaps altogether outside economics), from assuming a cardinal index of satisfaction, there is no reason why he should not assume it.[2] What does have to be maintained is that

[1] It will be evident to the reader how much this chapter owes to Sir Dennis Robertson, to his *Utility and All That* (1952) and 'Utility and All What?' (*Econ. Jour.* 1954). It is evident to the writer how much it owes to correspondence with Sir Dennis, going back to a much earlier date. I know that I shall not have convinced him, because I have here avoided the issues about which he cares most. But I myself do care about the issues I am discussing; otherwise I should not have written this book.

[2] It follows that the argument of this chapter leaves altogether on one side the vexed question about the use of a cardinal index in the Theory of Games; that issue is altogether separate from the one under discussion. I should however like to say that the assumption of a cardinal index, which appears to be a convenience in that theory, is evidently related to the assumption of measurable probabilities, which is necessary in that theory, but is a difficulty which stands in the way of its economic application. Whether the theory of games has much to offer the economist, in relation to the problem of risk, depends primarily, not on the measurability of utility, but on the measurability of risk itself. For my own part, I remain convinced by Knight's demonstration (in *Risk, Uncertainty and Profit*) that economic risks are ordinarily not measurable in the required sense. If this is accepted, the advantages of a cardinal assumption, even in risk theory, become very doubtful.

the special properties of a cardinal index are irrelevant to the econometric theory of consumers' behaviour. Concepts derived from these properties contain an element which is incapable of being used for the analysis of the market data with which the econometrist is concerned. A theory which is to provide the econometrist with tools which he can use, which is to ask questions which he is to have some hope of being able to answer, must, if it is based upon cardinal utility, extrude these cardinal properties before it reaches its conclusions. There would accordingly appear to be some presumption in favour of setting them on one side from the start.

Certainly the presumption is not overwhelming. It is possible that it might be more convenient to use the cardinal properties as a sort of scaffolding, useful in erecting the building, but to be taken down when the building has been completed. This is in fact what Marshall very largely did, and there is not in principle any objection to it. The objection is merely that in practice it does not seem to help. It is true that the more elementary parts of the theory can be established almost as well by the one method as by the other; but in the more difficult branches cardinal utility becomes a nuisance. I believe that this view will be impressed upon the reader by experience, if he penetrates to Part III of this book. But in the meantime it may be as well to indicate, in a more direct manner, just where the trouble lies.

2. In order to do this, let us make a little experiment. Let us make the cardinal assumption, apply it to market behaviour, and see where it leads us. In carrying out this experiment, we shall be obliged, in a certain sense, to duplicate the argument of succeeding chapters. It must therefore be emphasized that the present argument is solely directed at the question of the measurability of utility, and leads up to a negative conclusion. The positive argument of later chapters stands on its feet.

We must begin by distinguishing two possible forms of the cardinal hypothesis. The first, which has only to be mentioned in order to be rejected, is that of *independent* utilities. On this assumption, the utility which the consumer derives from each commodity purchased is a function of the quantity of that commodity, and of that commodity alone. The total utility of the whole collection of goods purchased is simply the sum of these separate utilities.

Giving this interpretation to the theory of Marshall, we should next say that the equilibrium of the consumer is determined by the well-known proportionality rule. The consumer, who has a fixed amount of money to spend, upon a market in which the prices of all commodities are given, will come to equilibrium at a position in which the marginal utility of each commodity is proportional to its price. This comes to the same thing, on the cardinal hypothesis, as saying that the marginal utility of each commodity is *equal* to its price multiplied by a common multiplier—the 'marginal utility of money'.

Now suppose that the price of one commodity (X) falls. If the purchases of all goods remained unchanged, the marginal utility of X would now be greater than its price multiplied by the marginal utility of money (assuming that the latter remains unchanged). In order to restore equilibrium, the consumption of X must accordingly increase. But when the demand for X has increased to such a point as makes the new marginal utility of X equal to the new price multiplied by the old marginal utility of money, the amount of money spent upon X is unlikely to remain unchanged; it may, however, either increase or diminish, according as the 'marginal utility curve' of X is elastic or inelastic. In order to restore total expenditure to the given amount which the consumer has available for spending, the marginal utility of money must be adjusted (upwards or downwards). If it is adjusted upwards, the marginal utilities of all commodities will become less than their prices multiplied by the new marginal utility of money; thus the demands for *all* commodities other than X (which had previously been left unadjusted) will tend to contract. If the adjustment is downwards, the demands for *all* other commodities than X will tend to expand. These conclusions are the inescapable consequence of the cardinal hypothesis with independent utilities.

Obviously they will not do. They imply that in all cases a reduction in the price of one commodity only will either result in an expansion in the demands for *all* other commodities, or in a contraction in the demands for all other commodities. The case, which ordinary experience suggests to be common, in which the demands for *some* other commodities expand while the demands for others contract, is excluded. In order to be able to deal with that case, we are obliged to reject the hypothesis of independent utilities.

3. The rejection is inevitable, but from the point of view of 'cardinalism' it is a serious matter. For if we were able to maintain independence, the way would be clear for the econometric determination of the main properties of the utility function. All we should have to do would be to find two situations, in which prices were different, in which different quantities of one commodity (call them x_1 and x_2) were consumed, but in which the same quantity (call it y) of another commodity was consumed. Then in the first situation the marginal utility of x_1 would be shown to be equal to the price-ratio between the commodities multiplied by the marginal utility of y; in the second situation the marginal utility of x_2 would be shown to be equal to the second price-ratio multiplied by the marginal utility of y; and the marginal utility of y (the quantity y being unchanged) would be the same in each case. The marginal utility of y would thus be available to act as a measuring-rod; in relation to that measuring-rod, we could measure the marginal utility of the commodity X. If we could find a series of such positions, in each of which the same quantity y was consumed, we could draw out a marginal utility curve for X. The scale of the curve would be unknown, since it would depend upon the unknown marginal utility of y; but its form (including, for instance, its elasticity) would be established. We might perhaps require to be lucky in order to hit upon a series of observations which exactly satisfied the above requirements; but it is clear that if independence is granted, marginal utility would be measurable in principle, and it is likely that indirect means could be found for measuring it in practice.[1] But all this depends upon independence.

For as soon as we contemplate the possibility that marginal utilities are interdependent, the above argument breaks down. It is then possible for the marginal utility of y to change, even though the consumption of the Y commodity does not change; it may change merely because the consumption of the X com-

---

[1] This is in fact what Ragnar Frisch tried to do in his *New Methods of Measuring Marginal Utility* (1932).

modity has changed from x_1 to x_2. The scale factor will thus cease to be constant. We shall cease to be able to measure the marginal utility of a commodity, even in the limited sense just described. All that we shall be able to measure is what the ordinal theory grants to be measurable—namely the ratio of the marginal utility of one commodity to the marginal utility of another.

4. Is it, however, not possible (an objector may ask) that out of the whole range of commodities other than X, there may be some which have marginal utilities that are affected by the quantity of X that is consumed, while there are others which have marginal utilities that are unaffected? All that would then need to be done, in order that a promising line of investigation should be salvaged, would be to take care that the commodity Y, chosen to act as a measuring-rod, was selected from the independent set, the dependent set being avoided. The difficulty about this escape is that it poses the problem of distinguishing the one set from the other. Common sense (or introspection) may indeed enable us to say that we should expect some particular Y to be a strong substitute (or complement) for the X we are considering; and that we should expect some other commodity Z to be weakly related to our X, if it is related at all. But how are we to have any confidence in the applicability of these hunches to the people whose behaviour we are trying to analyse? In particular, can we be sure that we can distinguish a commodity which is truly independent from one that is weakly (but significantly) substitutable? Surely these are questions which we ought not to have to answer from the inner light; they belong to the questions which we should be trying to answer from our empirical data.

If this is accepted, it follows that *theory* should not proceed upon the assumption that there are any goods with marginal utilities that are *necessarily* independent of the consumption of the good X. Any good *may* be related to X; it is up to us to show, from empirical data, whether it is or not. It follows that the direct measurement of marginal utilities, by the method we have been describing, must be judged to be out of reach. We do not possess a measuring-rod, in these matters, on the stability of which we can rely.

5. It does not, however, automatically follow that because we cannot measure marginal utility econometrically, we should

abandon its use as a conceptual tool. Though it cannot be measured itself, concepts which are based upon it (and its cardinal properties) may still be capable of being measured. In order to complete our test of the cardinal hypothesis, a further step is needed.

Let us therefore go back to our discussion of the effects of a single price-change, but now let us assume that utilities may be interdependent. That is to say, we now allow for the possibility that the marginal utility of any commodity may depend, not only upon the consumption of that commodity, but on the consumption of any other commodity purchased. We still assume that marginal utility is a cardinal magnitude, which is in principle capable of being measured.

When the price of X falls, the consumption of X increases, so as to make the new marginal utility of X equal to the reduced price multiplied by the marginal utility of money—just as before. But now, before considering the effect on the marginal utility of money, we must consider consequential effects on the marginal utilities of other commodities. The increased consumption of X will raise the marginal utilities of some other commodities, and will lower the marginal utilities of others. Consumption of the first set will accordingly rise—in order to restore equality between their marginal utilities and their prices (multiplied by the marginal utility of money); consumption of the second set will similarly fall.

But we have done no more so far than reach a stage of adjustment corresponding to the first stage of our analysis of independent utilities; there is still the effect on the marginal utility of money to be considered. As before, and for the same reason as before, the marginal utility of money may rise, or it may fall. If it falls, there will be a secondary expansion in the demands for most commodities, though not necessarily all (in view of interdependence); if it rises, there will be a secondary contraction. The total effect of the change in the price of X on the demand for Y (or for X itself) is a compound of the direct effect and of the indirect effect through the marginal utility of money.

This is the theory which emerges from the cardinal hypothesis, when it is logically followed through; but what are we to make of it? The distinction between direct and indirect effects of a price-change is unquestionably useful, and something very like it persists in the ordinal theory; but how, under cardinalism, do we separate out the two effects? Unless we can do so, we can have no proper theory of related commodities. For it is granted, under the above theory, that a fall in the price of X may increase the demand for Y without it being true that an increase in the consumption of X raises the marginal utility of Y; the increase in demand may have come about by a change in the marginal utility of money. How can we tell which of the two effects, or how much of each effect, has been responsible? We cannot even tell, if the cardinal theory is taken strictly, in what direction the marginal utility of money will have moved. This last difficulty could indeed be overcome if we could name certain other commodities as being independent of X, so that their demands could only be affected through the marginal utility; but we have seen that that is a thing which ought only to be done from market data, and cannot be done from market data. Even if it could be done, it would only get us part of the way along the road to the separation which we require.

The distinction between direct and indirect effects of a price-change is accordingly left by the cardinal theory as an empty box, which is crying out to be filled. But it can be filled. The really important thing which Slutsky discovered in 1915, and which Allen and I rediscovered in the nineteen-thirties,[1] is that content can be put into the distinction by tying it up with actual variations in income, so that the direct effect becomes the effect of the price-change combined with a suitable variation in income, while the indirect effect is the effect of an income change. In other words, the Marshallian distinction has been transmuted into the distinction between Substitution and Income Effects. In giving it this interpretation, we are not doing anything which is inconsistent with Marshall's theory, or at least with the essentials of that theory; but we are putting an edge upon it which was not there before.

It would not, I think, be denied, even by the most orthodox Marshallian, that in a case when a change in prices affects the marginal utility of money, there would be some change in income which would offset this latter effect, leaving the marginal

[1] 'A Reconsideration of the Theory of Value', *Economica*, 1934.

utility of money, as a result of the change in prices *and income*, the same as it was at the beginning. It follows that Marshall's division *is*, in some sense, a division between substitution and income effects. But what Marshall did not give us was a *rule* by which we could ascertain, in general, what the required change in income would be. It is, however, not at all difficult to find such a rule; once we have it, the theory which was incomplete can be completed.

Now as soon as we make our division in terms of a change in actual income, which does not need to be defined (nor does there look like being any call to define it) in terms of cardinal utility, we have in fact constructed a theory of demand the dependence of which upon cardinal utility is merely apparent. The direct (or substitution) effect is an effect on the marginal utilities of commodities, with the marginal utility of money constant; but that is in fact nothing else but an effect on the amount of *money* which the consumer is prepared to pay for a marginal unit of such a commodity. The indirect (or income) effect is the effect of a change in income, which again requires no utility analysis to explain it. Cardinalism has eliminated itself. Even if we start from cardinalism, we are bound to arrive, in the search for concepts which have a definable meaning, at something which is indistinguishable from an ordinal theory.

The above is nevertheless very far from being the best or most conclusive way of developing these concepts. We shall adopt a totally different route in the following chapters.

III

THE PREFERENCE HYPOTHESIS

1. The best way of approaching the econometric theory of demand is from the point of view of the empirical problem which throws up the need for such a theory.

The econometrist, who seeks to make a demand study, has before him something like the following situation. He is contemplating certain factual data, generally in the form of a time-series, showing the amounts of some commodity (or commodities) which have been purchased by a particular group of people during certain specified periods of time. His object is to find an explanation of these statistics, a hypothesis which will account for them. Common sense at once suggests a number of possible explanations, a number of lines on which an explanation may be sought. These may conveniently be classified in the following way.

First of all, there are the entirely non-economic (or perhaps it would be better to say, non-price) explanations—changes in population, age-distribution of population, social habits due to developments in housing and education, and so on. As causes of change these will rarely be unimportant, but they are less susceptible of economic analysis than those which come under the other heads. The second group will consist of price-explanations, explanations in terms of prices. We may include among these prices both the price (or prices) of the article (or articles) under consideration, and the prices of other articles—as well as the incomes of the consumers. I would, however, confine the prices to be reckoned under this second heading to current prices, prices ruling during the same period as that in which the commodities are purchased. Explanations in terms of the deferred, or lagged, effects of price-changes (such as may be particularly important with respect to durable goods) I would keep over for a third head.

The explanations on which we shall here concentrate attention are those which fall under the second heading, though this choice of subject involves no reflection upon the importance of the topics which would arise in a discussion of the third. Certainly the first thing which is asked of the econometrist is that he should estimate the effects which can be attributed to the various stimuli of the current-price type (estimates which may conveniently be shown in the form of elasticities). But in order for him to be able to make such estimates, he needs a technique for separating out the current-price effects from the others. Such a technique cannot be provided without a theory. The econometric purpose of the theory of demand is to give assistance in making this separation.

The kind of theory which is needed for this purpose is one which will tell us something about the ways in which consumers would be likely to react if variations in current prices and incomes were the only causes of changes in consumption. This is precisely what the theory of demand, considered from the econometric point of view, has to do. It proceeds by postulating an *ideal consumer*, who by definition is only affected by current market conditions, and asks how we should expect such a consumer to behave.

2. In order to get any answer to this question, we have to make some assumption about the principles governing his behaviour. The assumption of behaviour according to a scale of preferences comes in here as the simplest hypothesis, not necessarily the only possible hypothesis, but the one which, initially at least, seems to be the most sensible hypothesis to try. Its status is identically the same as that of a well-known class of hypotheses in natural science, hypotheses which cannot be tested directly, but which can be used for the arrangement of empirical data in meaningful ways, and which are accepted or rejected according to their success or failure as instruments of arrangement. There is no need to claim any more for it than this; but as a hypothesis of this sort, it seems to hold the field.[1]

---

[1] The modifications proposed by Professor J. S. Duesenberry (*Income, Saving, and the Theory of Consumer's Behaviour*) are in the nature of qualifications of the preference hypothesis, rather than a rejection of it. The same holds, I think, for those put forward by Mr. W. E. Armstrong. ('Determinateness of the Utility Function', *Econ. Journ.* 1939; 'Theory of Consumers' Behaviour', *Oxford Econ. Papers*, 1950.) It may well be that these qualifications are more relevant at the 'dynamic' stage of my third heading than at the 'static' stage with which I am here concerned. But whatever importance we attach to these qualifications, the full analysis of the preference hypothesis, in the sense defined above, is not made any the less necessary.

Certainly no simple alternative of equal fertility is available, none that is equally rich in consequences that can be empirically applied. Until we have an alternative that is equally usable, the Preference Hypothesis has to be (provisionally) accepted.

What I mean by action according to a scale of preferences is the following. The ideal consumer (who is not affected by anything else than current market conditions) chooses that alternative, out of the various alternatives open to him, which he most prefers, or ranks most highly. In one set of market conditions he makes one choice, in others other choices; but the choices he makes always express the same ordering, and must therefore be consistent with one another. This is the hypothesis made about the behaviour of the ideal consumer. Actual consumers will be affected by other things than by current prices, and their behaviour need not therefore always satisfy the tests of consistency. But if the hypothesis is justified, apparently inconsistent behaviour must be capable of explanation in terms of the ways in which the actual consumer differs from an ideal consumer; that is to say, it must be explicable in terms of changes in other variables than current prices (or income). The only way of testing the hypothesis is by seeing how far such explanations do in fact satisfy us, in the inconsistent cases which we find.

3. It would be possible, at this point, to proceed as I did in *Value and Capital*, expressing the given scale of preferences at once in the form of a set of indifference curves. This direct invocation of geometry has however several disadvantages. In the first place, geometry is fully effective as a means of demonstration only in quite simple cases, especially those in which the choice concerns quantities of two commodities only. As soon as we want to generalize, we have to fall back upon rather elaborate mathematics, which often tends to conceal the economic point of what is being done. A method which proceeds by short steps from one economically significant proposition to another, and uses geometry only for purposes of illustration, is technically much superior; such a method can now be found.

Another disadvantage of the geometrical method is that it forces us, at the start, to make assumptions of continuity, a property which the geometrical field does have, but which the economic in general does not. The ways in which the economic field exhibits discontinuity may not, in this matter of consumer's choice, be very important; but they are rather obvious, and it is a convenience if we do not have to begin by making the effort of assuming them away.

Neither of these disadvantages would however be sufficient in itself to justify the abandonment of a method which has its own advantages, and which economists have become accustomed to use. The consideration which decides me in favour of the new method, at least as an essential complement to the old, if not as a substitute, is its greater effectiveness in clarifying the nature of the preference hypothesis itself. The demand theory, which is based upon the preference hypothesis, turns out to be nothing else but an economic application of the logical theory of ordering; if we begin from the logic of ordering itself, instead of starting from the geometrical application of it, we begin by getting to our credit a number of distinctions, which will be of much use to us, and will save us from falling into some notorious pitfalls, later on.

4. The first of these distinctions is the distinction between two kinds of ordering. If a set of items is *strongly* ordered, it is such that each item has a place of its own in the order; it could, in principle, be given a number, and to each number there would be one item, and only one item, which would correspond. The letters of the alphabet are strongly ordered; so (with the one irregular exception of William and Mary) are the Kings of England. *Weak* ordering, on the other hand, allows for the possibility that some items may be incapable of being arranged in front of one another. Thus though the Parliaments of Great Britain are strongly ordered, the Members of Parliament (arranged by their dates of first election) are weakly ordered; for at each General Election a number of members are usually returned to the House for the first time. A weak ordering consists of a division into groups, in which the sequence of groups is strongly ordered, but in which there is no ordering within the groups.

Which kind of ordering is it that concerns us in demand theory? This is not so simple a question as may appear at first sight. The conventional 'indifference curve' diagram took it for granted that we were dealing with a weak ordering, with all the positions on the same indifference curve representing a non-ordered group. Some recent theory,[1] on the other hand, has appeared to assume strong ordering. It has done so for reasons which are closely connected with the general change in approach which we are accepting. It will however be useful to consider whether this particular change is a necessary consequence of the new approach.

It can, first of all, be admitted that one of the most awkward of the assumptions into which the older theory appeared to be impelled by its geometrical analogy was the notion that the consumer is capable of ordering all conceivable alternatives that might possibly be presented to him—all the positions which might be represented by points on his indifference map. This assumption is so unrealistic that it was bound to be a stumbling-block. From the new point of view it can be completely given up. All that we have to assume is that he can order those alternatives which he does actually have to compare in the situations under discussion—or, at the most, those which we might present to him, by a kind of hypothetical experiment, in the course of our argument. It is clearly a great advantage to be able to limit our assumption in this way. For the first part of the new condition is pretty easy to swallow; and as for the second, it is up to us to make it easy, by abstaining from the elaboration of arguments that rely upon difficult comparisons, or at the least by restraining ourselves from demanding much faith in the conclusions of such arguments. We can keep an eye upon the difficulty of the comparisons which are being invoked, and thus get a sense of the soundness or fragility of the plank on which we are walking.

Now if we are to think of the consumer as only ordering a finite, and perhaps quite small, number of alternatives, it is clearly possible that he may order them *strongly*, having a definite preference for A over B, B over C, and so on. It is not necessary that there should be any indifferent positions. Further, if the whole order is a strong one, it is sufficient to say that he always chooses the most preferred position open to him, and his choice is explained; preference is always sufficient to explain choice. If his ordering is weak, it is possible that there may be

[1] Samuelson, op. cit.; Little, *A Critique of Welfare Economics*, Ch. 2. While these writers do not deny the possibility of indifferent positions, they do assume that the positions between which choice is actually made can be strongly ordered.

two (or more) positions which stand together at the top of his list; choice between two such positions remains unexplained. The desire for a self-contained theory gives the economist some bias in favour of strong ordering.

But though this may be granted, it does not settle the question. The older theory may have exaggerated the omnipresence of indifference; but to deny its possibility is surely to run to the other extreme. It is surely the case that actual consumers do sometimes find themselves confronted with alternatives between which they are indifferent; if the ideal consumer is made incapable of being faced with such alternatives he is being made more unlike an actual consumers than he need be. If it is asked just what he will do when he is confronted with such alternatives, the answer must surely be that he will make a decision, but he will make it on grounds that have been excluded from consideration; his choice may depend, for instance, upon what he was doing *previously*. From the standpoint of a *static* theory, such as ours, such decision is a matter of chance. But chance, in this sense, is not a thing which ought to be excluded.

I am therefore of the opinion that demand theory, even in its new guise, ought to remain based upon weak ordering—chiefly for the reason that weak ordering is the less restrictive assumption. But we shall gain much by having a precise idea of the consequences of this decision. I shall therefore set out, in the following chapter, a sketch of the logical theory of both sorts of ordering; and I shall notice the differences between their consequences, as applied to economics, as I go on.

5. The other essential distinction which emerges from the logical analysis is that between Two-term Consistency Conditions and Transitivity Conditions. A preliminary account of this distinction may be given in the following way.

The function of the two-term consistency condition is to ensure that the relation between any two ordered items is unidirectional; it tells us that it is not possible for P to be above Q in the order, and for Q to be above P; P cannot be both above and below Q in the same order. It is evident from common sense, and will be verified in detail, that unless a relation exhibits two-term consistency it cannot be used for the construction of any sort of ordering. But it is not possible to build up a complete theory of ordering by using the two-term consistency condition alone. The other condition needed is one that can be taken for granted in many applications, so that it is easy to forget about it altogether. The simplest way of introducing it, and of showing that it really is necessary, is to take an example.

Suppose that we are trying to arrange in order a number of places on the Earth's surface; for simplicity, let us suppose that they all lie upon a single parallel of latitude, say the Equator. If the places are fairly near together, we can arrange them in order from east to west; one will be farthest east, another next farthest east, and so on, until we come to the last, which is farthest west. But if our places are scattered at random all round the Equator, we get into obvious difficulties. We can still arrange them in order, but only in a more limited sense. We cannot select any particular place as being farthest east; but, having selected at random some particular place, we can then arrange them in order *from that*, so that they go on getting farther west, until we come back to our starting-point. There is an order, but it is a 'circular' order, without top and bottom.

Now if we check through exactly what has happened in this 'circular' case, we find that it will first of all have been necessary to define 'east' and 'west' more precisely than we needed to do when the places were close together. Is the mouth of the Amazon east or west of the Island of Celebes? In order to answer this question in a workable manner, we must say that P is to the east of Q if it can be reached more rapidly by going eastwards from Q than by going westwards—which comes to the same thing as saying that it can be reached by going eastwards from Q *less than half-way round the world*. Without some such qualification, east and west have ceased to have a clear meaning.

Now the relation of east and west, on this interpretation, is perfectly satisfactory from the point of view of two-term consistency. Celebes is 170° to the east of the Amazon delta, but 190° to the west; thus it is unambiguously *east* of the Amazon. Whatever pair of places we take (unless they are one another's antipodes, and we will suppose that none of the places we are trying to order happen to have this peculiar relation), there is no danger of east and west getting mixed up. It is always true that if *P* is east of *Q*, *Q* is west of *P*. Yet though there is complete two-term consistency, we have not excluded 'circular' ordering.

What has gone wrong in the 'circular' case is that there is a failure of *transitivity*. The east–west relation will give us a proper unidirectional ordering so long as, in all the cases considered, the 'eastness' is transitive—so long as it is always true, when *P* is east of *Q*, and *Q* is east of *R*, that *P* is east of *R*. In our geographical instance this transitivity condition is satisfied for places that are near together, but not for places that are too far apart. Celebes (as we have seen) is *east* of the Amazon; Quito (being 160° farther east) is unambiguously *east* of Celebes; but it is not true that Quito (near the west coast of South America) lies to the east of the Amazon delta (on the east coast). Thus when we have a failure of transitivity, we may get the 'circular' case; it will be shown in the next chapter that transitivity, in conjunction with two-term consistency, is sufficient to ensure a complete, unidirectional, ordering.

6. It is one of the great advantages of the logical approach that it reduces the distinction just discussed into such manageable terms; for mathematical economics has made it quite unnecessarily mysterious. What corresponds to transitivity, in the mathematical theory, is *integrability*; a 'non-integrable' scale of preferences would be one that, at least in part, was circularly ordered.[1] In its mathematical form, the distinction looks rather worrying; but when it is put into its logical shape, there is surely no doubt at all what we should do with it. Since the preference hypothesis is only a hypothesis, we are at liberty to assume it in any form that we choose; but, that being so, there can surely be no doubt that it is the unidirectional form of the hypothesis which makes sense, not the circular form. It must be the unidirectional form that we want. It follows that the preferences of

[1] Thus, if there is non-integrability, some of the items which are being ordered may fall into an ordinary unidirectional order, while the remainder fall into a circularly ordered 'ring', or perhaps into several such rings. The limiting case of this latter possibility is that in which there is only one item in each ring; then [as will be explained in the next chapter] we have a situation in which no more than a limited number of the items which we are trying to order prove capable of being ordered. The remaining items have no order among themselves, and are incapable of being put into an ordered relation with the ordered items.

our consumer must not only exhibit two-term consistency, but also transitivity.

It is true that transitivity always involves three-term comparisons, as against the two-term comparisons involved in the other condition. It is also true that three-term comparisons are in general more difficult than two-term comparisons, so that an imperfect sense of order might conceivably take the form of an ability to make two-term comparisons, with an inability to go farther. But there is no obvious reason, in the economic setting, why an imperfect sense of ordering should take precisely this form. It seems much more plausible to assume that some sorts of multiple ordering are possible, but others are not possible. If we look at the matter in this way, we should in principle assume transitivity; but we should still endeavour to maintain a certain scepticism about some of the longer chains of comparison which we might be tempted to assume. That is the general attitude which the reader is invited to take to the ensuing chapters.

IV

THE LOGIC OF ORDER

1. Though the main distinctions in the logic of ordering which will concern us have already been described, I think it will be wise, before going farther, to set out the formal theory rather systematically. This is what I propose to do in the present chapter. It will involve us in a temporary excursion right outside the economic field, for we shall get a more reliable basis for our further investigations if we refrain from allowing ourselves to be influenced, at this stage, by the prospective application to economics. It will be better, for the present, to think of our problem as being one of the nature of ordering in general.[1]

We have a number of items before us which we seek to put into order. (Though the number may be large, it will be taken, for present purposes, to be always finite.) The first necessity, without which any sort of ordering is impossible, is that we should be able to select any item P, and should then be able to classify each other item according to the relation which subsists between that other item and P. Here at once we come up against the distinction between strong and weak ordering. If the ordering is to be strong, all items other than P will have to be *either* before P *or* after P, when the ordering is achieved. Thus, at this stage, it will be necessary that all items other than P should be classifiable into two classes, one consisting of items having one sort of relation to P, the other of items having a different sort of relation. With strong ordering, these two classes must satisfy the following conditions: (*a*) they must include all items other than P, and (*b*) they must not overlap, so that there are any items in both classes. I call these two conditions the *Preliminary Conditions* of Strong Ordering.

If, on the other hand, the ordering is to be weak, then there may be items other than P which will not come before P *or*

---

[1] I have been much influenced in this chapter by the work of K. J. Arrow (*Social Choice and Individual Values*, ch. 2), though I have not followed him in all respects.

after P in the ordering. This situation can be met, in terms of the preliminary conditions, by dropping *one or the other* of the preliminary conditions of strong ordering. Thus we may either say that the two classes, which are to become 'before' and 'after', do not between them include all items other than P, so that the first of the preliminary conditions of strong ordering is dropped; or we may say that there are two classes, which are to become 'not after' and 'not before', which do contain all items other than P, but which may overlap, so that the second of the preliminary conditions of strong ordering is dropped. It is a matter of taste which of these two approaches we adopt; but in either case there is only *one* Preliminary Condition of Weak Ordering, as against the *two* conditions of strong ordering. This distinction serves to define the difference between the two cases.

2. Let us, for the present, confine our attention to strong ordering, and proceed to elaborate that (at this stage slightly easier) theory. We may then say that we have started from a 'basis' P, and have divided *all* the remaining items into two mutually exclusive classes, which we will call 'items left of P' and 'items right of P' respectively. Notice that we have not yet shown that these items can remain left of P and right of P in any final ordering; the arrangement which has so far been made is solely *with respect to the basis P*. In order to get something more than this preliminary classification, we have got to establish that classifications with respect to different bases are consistent with one another.

Take a different basis Q, and classify the other items with respect to Q. It is natural to begin by asking whether P and Q are consistently placed with respect to each other's classifications. This gives us the *two-term consistency conditions*:

(1) If Q is left of P, P must be right of Q.
(2) If Q is right of P, P must be left of Q.

These two conditions are of the same form, but I prefer to write them as two conditions, not one. For in any particular application, it is quite possible that one condition might hold, but not the other. Both conditions are necessary for a complete and consistent ordering.

Let us look at some examples. Suppose that our *items* are

people, and that 'items left of P' are people who are brothers to P, while 'items right of P' are people who are not brothers to P. This classification satisfies the preliminary conditions of strong ordering, but it falls down on either of the two-term consistency conditions. For if Q is left of P, he is a brother to P, so that P is a brother to Q, and is left of Q, instead of being right of Q as he should be if the first consistency condition is to be satisfied. And if Q is right of P, he is not a brother to P, so that P is not a brother to Q, and is right of Q, whereas he should be left of Q is the second consistency condition was to be satisfied. Thus the relationship of 'brotherhood' (sans phrase) breaks down on both of the two-term consistency conditions.

But now suppose that 'items left of P' are people who are *elder brothers* of P, while 'items right of P' are people who are *not elder brothers* of P, whether they are brothers at all or not. Now if Q is left of P, he is an elder brother of P; P is therefore not an elder brother of Q, and is right of Q, as he should be in accordance with the first consistency condition. But if Q is right of P, he is not an elder brother of P; if in fact he was a younger brother, P would be left of Q, and the second consistency condition would be satisfied. But for all we have said, there is no reason why he should be a younger brother; he might not be a brother at all. If so, Q would be right of P, but P would be right of Q; so that the second consistency condition would break down. Thus if one consistency condition is satisfied but not the other, we can order some of the items in our set (such as those who happen to be 'brothers') but not the rest. For a complete ordering we need both conditions.

3. Even if both of the two-term consistency conditions are satisfied, for every possible pair $P\ Q$, it is however still not true that the whole set of items is necessarily capable of being ordered in a straightforward unidirectional manner. For the possibility of 'circular' ordering (as in the *equatorial* example of the previous chapter) has still to be ruled out. Putting the same point in another way, we have ensured that P and Q are consistently ordered with respect to one another; but we have not ensured that the whole classification with respect to P is consistent with the whole classification with respect to Q. It is for this purpose that we need the further condition, which is the Transitivity condition.

Though the transitivity condition can be written in either of two forms, which correspond to the *two* consistency conditions, there is only one transitivity condition, not two; for one of the two forms follows from the other. In order to show this, let us assume the transitivity condition in its 'left' form, which says that

If Q is left of P, and R is left of Q, R is left of P (P, Q, R being distinct items).

Now if this is true, and the two-term consistency conditions are also true, we can argue as follows:

If P is right of Q, and Q is right of R,
then Q is left of P, and R is left of Q (2nd consistency cdn.),
then R is left of P (transitivity cdn.),
then P is right of R (1st consistency cdn.).

So that the transitivity condition also holds in its 'right' form. Thus we do not need more than one independent transitivity condition.

We have seen just what it is that goes wrong if we try to carry out a strong ordering with less than all of these necessary[1] conditions. But we have still to show that the conditions which we have listed are sufficient to establish a complete ordering. This may be shown in the following way.

Suppose that we have a set of items, between which all the conditions, which we have been listing, hold. We may then take any item P as a basis, and divide all the remaining items into those which are 'left' and those which are 'right' of P. We can

---

[1] The necessary conditions for strong ordering could indeed have been grouped in different ways from that which we have chosen. If, for instance, we had taken the transitivity condition without the qualification that P, Q, R must be distinct items, we could have deduced the first consistency condition from the *left* form of the transitivity condition, so that we could have dispensed with the first consistency condition. For we could then have argued, from the transitivity condition, that

If Q is left of P, and P is left of Q, P is left of P;

and this is impossible, since items left of P have been defined to be distinct from P. Thus, P Q being distinct, it is impossible that Q can be left of P and P left of Q; so that if Q is left of P, P must be right of Q. But if we had adopted this method, we should have been unable to deduce the second form of the transitivity condition from the first; so that we should have been obliged to maintain two independent transitivity conditions. Thus our gain would not have been very great.

The reasons which have led me to prefer the arrangement given in the text will become apparent when we pass on to the *weak* theory.

next take any item Q among those which are left of P, and divide all items other than Q into those which are left of Q and those which are right of Q. We shall know (by two-term consistency) that P is one of the items which are right of Q. And we shall also know (by transitivity) that any item which is left of Q must be left of P; and (by the other form of the transitivity condition) that any item which is right of P must be right of Q. Thus we have divided the whole set of items (other than P and Q) into three sub-sets

(1) those which are left of Q, and therefore left of P,
(2) those which are right of P, and therefore right of Q,
(3) the remainder (if any).

These remaining items are not left of Q, and are therefore right of Q; they are not right of P, and are therefore left of P; thus they are definable as those items (if any) which are right of Q and left of P. The three sub-sets have accordingly been arranged in order, from left to right.

We can then go on to select a third 'basis' item (R), which must itself lie in one of the three sub-sets. If R is left of Q, so that it lies in the first sub-set, then all items which are left of R must (by transitivity) be left of Q; R will therefore divide the first sub-set into those items which are left of itself, and those which are right of itself but left of Q. It will make similar divisions if it comes into the other sub-sets. The three *bases* will accordingly divide the whole set into four sub-sets which are in order; no new condition is needed for this to occur.

The same process can be continued, by the introduction of additional bases, until the whole set has been ordered. Thus the whole theory of strong ordering depends upon no more than the preliminary conditions, the two-term consistency conditions, and the transitivity condition which have been laid down.

4. Let us now proceed to examine the theory of weak ordering in a similar way. Since the other items are now to be classified, with respect to any basis, into three non-overlapping groups, instead of two, we must expect to find that the theory of weak ordering is a little more complicated than the theory of strong ordering. It can, however, be set out in a similar manner, with exactly corresponding parts.

First of all, as we saw, with weak ordering we have only one preliminary condition, not two. But since we have a choice which of the preliminary conditions of strong ordering we shall drop, the theory of weak ordering can be put into either of two alternative forms, which are equally valid. We may on the one hand say that with respect to any basis P, the remaining items are classifiable into *three* non-overlapping classes: 'items left of P', 'items right of P' and 'items neither left nor right of P'. The analysis which is based upon this threefold classification I shall call the *positive form* of weak theory. Alternatively, we may say that with respect to any basis P, the remaining items are classifiable into *two* possibly overlapping classes: 'items not right of P' and 'items not left of P'. The analysis which is based upon this I shall call the *negative form* of the theory.

Each of the two forms proceeds by the enumeration of two-term consistency conditions, and transitivity conditions, as before. So long as we are concerned with the two-term consistency conditions, the distinction between the two forms is of little importance. In either form, we have a pair of two-term conditions (as before); though they are written in different ways in the two forms, the one pair is exactly equivalent to the other; one follows from the other. But when we go on to transitivity, there is a divergence. The *negative form* of the weak theory can be built up from one transitivity condition alone, as the strong theory is. But the *positive form* is less efficient, since it requires two transitivity conditions. (It must however be admitted that this is something of a trick, since all that has happened is that the terminology of the negative form enables us to bring the two conditions of the positive form under a single umbrella.)

5. If we take the positive form, the two-term consistency conditions will be written just as they are written in the strong theory:

(1) If Q is left of P, P is right of Q.

(2) If Q is right of P, P is left of Q.

As before, neither of these follows from the other. But it does follow from the first condition that

(1') If P is not right of Q, Q is not left of P,

and from the second that

(2') If P is not left of Q, Q is not right of P,

and these are the two-term conditions in their negative form. Thus if the 'positive' conditions hold for all pairs of P and Q, the 'negative' conditions will hold for all pairs. And if we had begun from the 'negative' conditions, we could have deduced the 'positive' conditions in a similar way. The two pairs are exactly equivalent.

We can go on to observe that in the case of weak ordering, there is a further important deduction to be drawn from two-term consistency. This follows at once from the negative form of the two-term conditions. It is now possible that P may be 'neither left nor right' of Q; or, as we shall say for brevity, it is 'neutral to Q'. Then, if P is neutral to Q, it follows from the two-term conditions, in their negative form, that Q is neutral to P. For we have only to take the two 'negative' conditions together, and the result follows.

Thus 'neutrality' is reversible, and the unclassified items are brought into some sort of relation with one another. But they are not yet brought into any relation with the ordering that is emerging. This can readily be shown by an extension of the illustration which we used a little earlier. Suppose that items left of P are elder brothers of P, items right of P are younger brothers, items neutral to P are not brothers at all. Then the two 'positive' conditions tell us that (1) if Q is an elder brother of P, P is a younger brother of Q; (2) if Q is a younger brother of P, P is an elder brother of Q; both of which statements are agreeable to common sense. The corresponding 'negative' conditions are equally intelligible, as of course they must be. But all that we learn, in this case, from the reversibility of neutrality, is that if P is not a brother to Q, Q is not a brother to P; this again is perfectly true, but it does nothing to establish any sort of family connexion. Even if we allowed for the possibility that 'neutral items' might be twins, we should have no means of separating the twins from those who are not members of the family. We do not get that until we come to transitivity.

6. When we come to transitivity, there is (as was stated) an advantage to be got from using the negative form, since we can then make do with *one* transitivity condition. Let us write it

If Q is not right of P, and R is not right of Q, R is not right of P.

As in the case of strong ordering, the fellow of this can be deduced from it (by using the two-term conditions in their negative form). For

If P is not left of Q, and Q is not left of R,
then Q is not right of P, and R is not right of Q
                                    (2nd consistency cdn.),
then R is not right of P (transitivity cdn.),
then P is not left of R (1st consistency cdn.).

And there are numerous other consequences which can be deduced.

In the first place, we can deduce the *transitivity of neutrality*.

'If P is neutral to Q, and Q is neutral to R, P is neutral to R.'

This follows at once from the two basic transitivity conditions just stated.

Secondly, we can deduce the transitivity conditions in their positive form. Each is, of course, proved the same way; let us take the case of 'leftness'.

'If P is left of Q, and Q is left of R, P is left of R.'

We prove this by showing that the opposite is impossible. If P is left of Q, then (by the two-term consistency condition in its positive form) Q is right of P. But if Q is right of P, then (by the preliminary condition which remains with us) Q is not left of P. Thus, if the above conclusion were not true, so that P was not left of R, we should have P not left of R, and Q not left of P; whence (by the transitivity condition in its negative form) Q is not left of R. But Q is left of R, so that we have come to a contradiction. Thus the proposition is established.

Finally, we can deduce a group of important propositions which we shall call *gearing* propositions, because they have the effect of bringing the unclassified items into relation with the system of ordering that is emerging. These are all of the same form and are proved in the same way. Let us take as an example

'If P is neutral to Q, and Q is left of R, then P is left of R.' Here, if P is neutral to Q, Q is neutral to P (by the reversibility of neutrality); hence Q is not left of P (by the definition of neutrality). Hence if the above proposition were not true, and P was not left of R in the conditions stated, we should have Q not left of P, and P not left of R, so that Q would be not left of R (by the transitivity condition in its negative form). But Q is left of R, so that again we have a contradiction. Thus the proposition is established.

We accordingly learn that an item which is not ordered with respect to Q is nevertheless ordered with respect to such items as are ordered with respect to Q. Wholly unordered items will not occur. As we saw, such unrelatedness is not excluded by the two-term conditions, when we are working under the single preliminary condition of weak ordering; it takes transitivity to exclude it. Now it may at first sight seem surprising that the transitivity condition, when taken in its negative form, is sufficient to exclude unrelatedness; and it will be well to pause for a moment to see why this is. A reference to our usual example will in fact serve to clear the matter up.

If, as before, items left of P are elder brothers of P, and items right of P are younger brothers of P, while items neutral to P are not brothers at all, then (as we saw) the two-term consistency conditions will all be satisfied. But the (negative) transitivity condition now says that if P is not an elder brother of Q, and Q is not an elder brother of R, P will not be an elder brother of R. On the interpretation we are giving, that is not necessarily true. It is possible that P may be an elder brother of R, even though Q is not a member of the same family, so that he is unrelated to either of them. But the transitivity condition would be necessarily true, if our 'items' were all brothers, even though there was some twinning in the family. Thus as soon as the transitivity condition is satisfied for all triads in the set, it does follow that all items are brought into relation with a single ordering.

All these propositions follow from a single transitivity condition, so long as that condition is taken in its negative form. If, however, we had started from the positive form of the transitivity condition, we could have proved the transitivity of 'rightness' from that of 'leftness'; but none of the rest would have followed. It would have been impossible, in the first place, to prove the transitivity of neutrality; for that would not follow from the two *positive* conditions. In fact, if we had started from the positive form, there would have been nothing for it but to introduce the transitivity of neutrality as an independent assumption. Once that was granted, the rest would indeed follow. But I think that I may leave the proof of this last statement as an exercise for the reader.[1]

7. We have now accumulated all the conditions which are necessary for the establishment of a system of weak ordering. As in the strong case, we start from a basis P, and classify all other items with respect to P. This gives us three classes of items: (1) items left of P, (2) items neutral to P, (3) items right of P. We then select a second basis Q, which must fall into one or another of the classes just listed. Suppose, to begin with, that Q is right of P. Then (by the two-term condition) P is left of Q; and (by the transitivity of leftness) any item which is left of P must be left of Q. It also follows from the gearing proposition stated (with an appropriate change of lettering) that any item which is neutral to P must be left of Q. A corresponding proposition of the same type will tell us that any item which is neutral to Q must be right of P, while the transitivity of rightness tells us that any item which is right of Q must be right of P. Thus the two bases separate the whole set into five sub-sets:

(1) those items which are left of P (and therefore left of Q),
(2) those items which are neutral to P (and therefore left of Q),
(3) those which are neutral to Q (and therefore right of P),
(4) those which are right of Q (and therefore right of P),

together with a remainder, included in none of these four, which must consist of items right of P and left of Q.

The case in which Q is left of P is exactly the same, *mutatis mutandis*, and needs no further attention. That in which Q is neutral to P deserves formal presentation. If Q is neutral to P, two-term consistency shows that P is neutral to Q; while the

---

[1] It will now be apparent that if we had proceeded, in the construction of the weak theory, on the lines of the footnote on p. 28, we should have been obliged to build up the two-term conditions from two independent transitivity conditions (for 'leftness' and 'rightness') in their *positive* form. The negative form would have been no good, for if P is not left of P there is no contradiction. But from the two *positive* transitivity conditions we could not deduce the transitivity of neutrality, so that that condition would have had to be introduced as an independent assumption. Thus from *three* transitivity conditions, without independent two-term conditions, the whole of the weak theory could have been built up. But we should have got no gain in economy by that route, and less insight into the structure of the system.

transitivity of neutrality shows that any item which is neutral to P is neutral to Q, and vice versa. The gearing proposition shows us that if P is neutral to Q, and Q is left of R, P is left of R; so that any item which is right of Q is right of P. Another gearing proposition will show us that any item which is left of Q is left of P. In this case, then, we have only three classes: (1) items left of P and Q, (2) items neutral to P and Q, (3) items right of P and Q. The bases P and Q give the same classification.

We can now continue, as in the case of strong ordering, with the introduction of additional bases, until the ordering is complete. The propositions already established enable us to fit every item into a consistent place, no new conditions being required.

This is all that needs to be said, for our purposes, about the logic of ordering. We are now equipped to turn to the economic application.

V

STRONG AND WEAK ORDERING IN
DEMAND THEORY

1. I propose to make considerable use, in this and the following chapters, of a device which I introduced in *Value and Capital*. It is always possible, in any problem of demand theory (an analogous simplification can be used in any department of economics) to treat a group of commodities, which are such that their price-ratios remain constant throughout the situations under discussion, as if they were a single commodity. This statement does not require any mathematical proof; it is securely based upon economic common sense. It can be quite sufficiently established in the following way.

If we consider the wants of a consumer who is purchasing, in the period under consideration, a wide variety of commodities, and treat him as an ideal consumer with a fixed scale of preferences, we can obviously embody in his system of preferences the fact that some of the commodities he is purchasing will have a variety of *uses*. If he buys more of one commodity (say electricity) in one situation than in another, he may well divide the electricity which he is purchasing in different proportions among these uses in the two situations. But unless we are specially interested in the distribution among uses, we need not show this distribution explicitly in our study of his behaviour. It will be sufficient if we show him purchasing such and such quantities of electricity at such and such prices, and leave it at that.

The case in which the price-ratios of a group of commodities remain constant is analytically identical. We can construct a generalized commodity, in terms of which the prices of the whole group of goods will remain completely constant; we can then study the demand for the generalized commodity in exactly the same way as we should have studied the demand for electricity in the previous example. So far as the behaviour of our consumer is concerned, the exchange of the generalized commodity for the particular commodities which replace it is exactly analogous to the distribution of the electricity among its uses. When we are engaged on the study of demand for commodities outside the group, the exchange of the generalized commodity for its 'components' may be regarded as a separate operation, with which we are only indirectly concerned. Unchanged opportunities for further exchange may be regarded as being embodied in the unchanged scale of preferences which we are studying.

In the exposition of demand theory, this principle has one particularly simple, and particularly important, application. If we are studying the effects of changes in the price of one commodity only, so that the prices of all the other commodities which are purchased are to remain constant, we can treat all these other commodities as if they were a single commodity. Thus the study of the effects of price-changes for a single commodity can be reduced to a study of the choice between *two* commodities—the commodity which we shall call X, the price of which varies in the course of discussion, and the generalized commodity M, which represents all other commodities taken together. Thus the study of *simple* price-changes (as we shall call them) reduces to a study of the behaviour of a consumer who spends all his income on *two goods*.

I think that the above argument is now generally accepted; but it is worth noticing, before we proceed to apply it, that it throws a curious light upon a famous episode in the history of demand theory—the difference between Marshall and Pareto. Marshall based his theory (in Book III of the *Principles*) on a study of *simple* price-changes—the demand curve for a single commodity. Pareto sought to generalize, and in his mathematical theory he did generalize; but his diagrammatic analysis—the indifference curve diagram which symbolizes his theory to his readers as the demand curve does Marshall's—shows the consumer dividing his expenditure between two goods. Now it appears from the above that the only practical situation, to which such two-good analysis can be applied, is precisely the case which was analysed by Marshall. In order to make use of Pareto's diagram (once again, I do not speak of his mathematical theory) we have to interpret the two goods as being X (the good whose price is changing) and M (the composite commodity).

So interpreted, the Pareto diagram provides a useful alternative approach to Marshall's problem; but it is the same problem which is being studied in both cases. In order to go farther, we have to use other methods.

2. On this interpretation, it is perfectly realistic to begin our discussions with the consideration of the behaviour of a consumer who is spending his income on two commodities. This is the way in which all demand theories (save those which are purely mathematical) have in fact begun; and we now see that it is the correct way to begin. Initially, the consumer is confronted with given prices for both commodities; he has a given amount of money to spend, which (in a static theory of our sort) may, without danger of misunderstanding, be called his *income*. He can buy as much as he likes (or can afford) of each commodity at its given price; thus there is no rationing, and the market is perfectly competitive from the consumer's point of view. Most markets at most times do satisfy these conditions; the exceptional markets which do not will not be studied in the present work.

Since any other use for money (or income) save spending it upon X is supposed to be included in the composite commodity M, it is obviously correct to think of the consumer as spending all his income—not spending it could have no meaning save throwing it away. (Saving it for the future would be included in the composite commodity.) It will, however, be an analytical convenience if we leave our consumer at liberty to throw his money away if he likes; though we may accept it as an observed fact that the representative consumer does not do so in practice.

Let us next proceed to represent the situation so described upon a simple diagram (Fig. 1)—an adaptation of the Paretian diagram which has become famous. If we measure quantities of the two goods (X and M) along the two axes, any point on the diagram will represent a pair of quantities of the two goods. With given prices, and given income, the quantities available to the consumer are limited by a straight line such as *aa*, which is such that the slope of the line measures the ratio between the prices of the two goods, and the intercepts (Oa) on the axes measure the quantity of either good which could be acquired if none of the other good were to be purchased. The available alternatives are then represented by points within the triangle *aOa*, or by points on the boundary of the triangle. Any point on *aa* represents a situation in which the whole of income is being spent on the two goods, and we are to suppose that the point actually selected (*A*) lies on this line. Supposing that our consumer is an ideal consumer, who is acting according to the preference hypothesis, how is this conduct to be interpreted?

It is at this point that we must be careful to distinguish be-

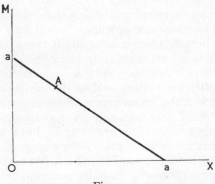

Fig. 1.

tween the two forms of the preference hypothesis. If the available alternatives are *strongly ordered*, we can say that our consumer shows that he prefers the alternative selected over any other alternative open to him and rejected: which means that he prefers the position *A* to any other position within or on the triangle. In Samuelson's language, he 'reveals his preference' for *A* over the rejected positions. Thus we get a definite piece of information about his preferences from the observation of his behaviour; by comparing the preferences 'revealed' in different price- and income-situations certain information about his preference scale can be built up.

Strong ordering gets off to a racing start; but even at the outset there are certain snags about it which deserve attention. If we interpret the preference hypothesis to mean strong ordering, we can hardly assume that all the geometrical points, which lie

within or on the triangle aOa, represent effective alternatives.
The natural assumption for this case is that the commodities
are only available in discrete units, so that the diagram is to be
thought of as being drawn on squared paper, and the only
effective alternatives are the points at the corners of the squares.
The point A itself must evidently lie at a square-corner.[1]

On this interpretation, the strong ordering hypothesis is
acceptable; but the interpretation itself gives one some qualms.
It is quite true that the actual commodities purchased by actual
consumers are usually sold in discrete units; you cannot buy a
fraction of an electric lamp, and (unless compelled by a rationing
authority) shopkeepers are unwilling to sell very odd fractions
of a pound of butter. Thus it is intelligible that the actual commodity X, which we are measuring along the horizontal axis of
our diagram, should only be available in an integral number of
units. But does the same thing hold for the composite commodity
M? If every one of the actual commodities into which M can be
exchanged is itself only available in discrete units, then (in a
sense) M is only available in discrete units; but if the number of
such commodities is large, there will be a large number of ways
in which a small increment of M can be consumed by rearrange-
ment of consumption among the individual commodities, whence
it will follow that the units in which M is to be taken to be available must be considered as exceedingly small. And as soon as
any individual commodity becomes available in units that are
finely divisible, M must be regarded as finely divisible. In
practice, we should usually think of M as being money, held
back for the purchase of other commodities than X; though
money is not finely divisible in a mathematical sense, the smallest
monetary unit (farthing or cent) is so small in relation to the
other units with which we are concerned that the imperfect
divisibility of money is in practice a thing of no importance. For
these reasons, while it is a theoretical improvement to be able

---

[1] It is not true, as was stated in the original edition of this book, that 'a two-
dimensional continuum cannot be strongly ordered'. It is nevertheless true
that it cannot be strongly ordered except in some such manner as the 'striped
diagram' (Fig. 2) can be strongly ordered; and this, as we shall see, is an
alternative that must be rejected. (See Note A, p. 195.)

to regard the actual commodity X as available in discrete units, it is no improvement at all to be obliged to impute the same indivisibility to the composite commodity M. It is much better to regard M as finely divisible.

But if we do that, we cannot maintain the strong form of the preference hypothesis. For the effective alternatives are now no longer represented by square-corners; they will appear on the diagram as a series of parallel lines (or stripes) as shown in

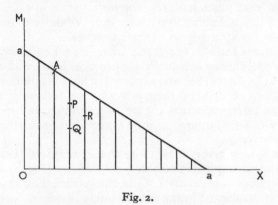

Fig. 2.

Fig. 2. Any point on one of these stripes is an effective alternative. Now such alternatives as these cannot be strongly ordered, unless the *whole* of one stripe was preferred to the *whole* of the next stripe, and so on; which means that the consumer would always prefer an additional unit of X, whatever he had to pay for it—though he would prefer a larger amount of M to a smaller, if the amount of X which he had was unchanged. This assumption is nearly nonsensical, and can be ruled out. If, on the other hand, there are two points P, Q on the same stripe, which are such that P is preferred to R on another stripe, while R is preferred to Q, we could always find a point between P and Q which was indifferent to R, so that we could not maintain strong ordering. As soon as we introduce the smallest degree of continuity (such as is introduced by the 'striped' hypothesis), strong ordering has to be given up.

3. Let us therefore turn to examine the weak ordering

alternative, which (as we admitted) is at first sight less promising. If the consumer's scale of preferences is weakly ordered, then his choice of a particular position A (Fig. 1) does not show (or 'reveal') that A is preferred to any rejected position within or on the triangle; all that is shown is that there is no rejected position which is preferred to A. It is perfectly possible that some rejected position may be indifferent to A; the choice of A instead of that rejected position is then (as we saw) a matter of 'chance'. Thus we learn much less from the observation of actual data, if we adopt the preference hypothesis in its weak form, than we do if we take the strong form of the hypothesis.

Indeed, we learn so much less when we take the weak form, that we could make absolutely no progress at all without some further help. As will become apparent in later chapters, the basic propositions of demand theory would not follow, if we were unable to interpret actual choice as providing any more than this very negative information. We must have something more to get any farther.

But it is only a very little more that is required. Let us take the conditions implied in our 'striped' diagram (Fig. 2), in which the composite commodity (M) is finely divisible, though the actual commodity (X) may not be finely divisible. Let us now introduce the *additional* hypothesis, that the consumer will always *prefer* a larger amount of M to a smaller amount of M, provided that the amount of X at his disposal is unchanged. It must be emphasized that this is an additional hypothesis, which does not need to be made if we can assume strong ordering. But it is an exceedingly reasonable hypothesis, which has frequently slipped into economic analysis without having any special attention drawn to it. But attention should be drawn to it, if we are to realize what we are doing—so that we can be clear, at later stages of our analysis, what it is that we have a right to do.

Let us examine what is the effect of the weak ordering hypothesis, fortified with this additional assumption. Under weak ordering, the fact that position A (Fig. 3) is selected, instead of position B, which is within the triangle, does not itself tell us that A is preferred to B; all it does tell us is that B is not preferred to A. That is, either A is preferred to B, or A and B are indifferent. But now consider a position L, which lies at the intersection of the line *aa*, and of the stripe through *B*. Under the assumptions we are making, *L* is a possible alternative. *L* is preferred to *B*, by the additional hypothesis. Thus if *A* and *B* are indifferent, it will follow from the transitivity of weak ordering[1] that *L* is preferred to *A*. But *L* is itself one of the positions which has been rejected in favour of *A*; though it may be indifferent to *A*, it cannot be preferred to *A*. Thus the alternative that *A* and *B* are indifferent must be ruled out.

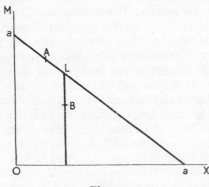

Fig. 3.

Thus it is possible to prove, even under weak ordering, when we add the additional assumption, that the position actually selected is preferred over any position that lies *within* the triangle. What cannot be shown, by this reasoning, is that *A* is preferred over *L*, that the chosen position is preferred over another position, which also lies on the line *aa*. The difference between the consequences of strong and weak ordering, so interpreted, amounts to no more than this: that under strong ordering the chosen position is shown to be preferred to all other positions *in* and *on* the triangle, while under weak ordering it is preferred to all positions *within* the triangle, but may be indifferent to other positions on the same boundary as itself.

4. This difference between the effects of the two hypotheses is, of course, very slight; it merely affects a class of limiting

[1] Strictly, from the gearing proposition which is a consequence of transitivity (see above, p. 32).

cases. The weak theory has a larger tolerance, and therefore (as we shall see) it deals with these limiting cases rather better. But it is not for the sake of the limiting cases that I have gone to the trouble of a separate elaboration of the two theories. We shall derive a much wider benefit from a recognition of the fact that there are these two alternative approaches, and from an exact appreciation of the assumptions upon which each is based.

If we take the strong ordering approach, we are committing ourselves to discontinuity; not merely to the indivisibility of the particular commodity, demand for which is being studied, but also to indivisibility of the composite commodity used as background. If, on the other hand, we take the weak ordering approach, we are committing ourselves to some degree of continuity—but divisibility of the background commodity is itself quite sufficient to ensure that the weak approach is practicable. We have, however, also learned that the weak approach requires an additional assumption, to which there is no parallel in the strong case: we have to assume that marginal units of the background commodity are positively desired—or, as the older theory would say, that the background commodity has a positive marginal utility. We have further to assume that the preference order is transitive, even at this early stage of our investigation.

I do not myself feel that these assumptions, which are necessary for the weak theory, are at all hard to swallow; they seem to be a very reasonable price for the advantages which they bring. But it is very useful indeed to have discovered that these assumptions are necessary at the very start of the weak approach; we are already committed to them when we start on that tack, so that we need have no compunction in making use of them again later on. Some of the doubts which economists have sometimes felt about these assumptions thus turn out to have been due to an inadequate appreciation of the distinction between strong and weak theory. If we are using the strong hypothesis, we can do without these extra assumptions, but we must then take all the consequences of the strong hypothesis; if, on the other hand, we prefer the weak route, we are entitled to use *all* the assumptions upon which the weak route must be based.

So far, in this chapter, I have considered the two hypotheses in terms of the choice between two goods, which (as was explained) is the appropriate framework when we are interested in the demand for a single commodity. The same argument can readily be extended to more complex problems, for most of the problems of multiple price-changes are reducible to a similar pattern. Instead of spot-lighting a single commodity X, we now spot-light a number of different commodities X, Y, Z, and so on; but we should still think of these commodities as being put against a background—of 'money' available for spending on anything not explicitly included in the list. As the list of commodities explicitly considered grows longer, the scope of the background commodity becomes narrower; the arguments for treating it as being finely divisible do then become gradually less compelling. But it is only in the extreme case (which in application is a very extreme case) when nearly all the commodities currently consumed are brought into the foreground, that the argument from the spreading of 'money' over a group of actual commodities ceases to apply. In that case, if we want to use weak ordering, we have to rely upon some actual commodity[1] being finely divisible, or divisible into units which are so small that their indivisibility can be neglected. If such a commodity can be found (I do not myself think that it would be so very hard to find it), it can perform the function which has been performed by the background commodity in the preceding argument. Thus even when we go to the extreme, the weak approach can still be saved; but it is not often that it is necessary to go to such an extreme. Most of the applications we desire to make[2] will leave us with a 'background' which is quite sufficient.

The way in which we shall now proceed to arrange our discussion is at once suggested by the argument of this chapter. We shall begin (in Part II) with the two-good case, for the study of which we can stick closely to Marshallian and Paretian precedent. We shall follow that through, making strict application of the preceding principles, so that the consequences of the strong ordering approach, and of the weak ordering approach, are clearly distinguished. In this study of the two-good case, we shall be able to make full use of the traditional geometry; but we shall sometimes use Marshall-type, and sometimes Pareto-type

---

[1] Which may—or may not—be one of those which are spot-lighted.
[2] See, however, Ch. XIX.

diagrams, just as seems at the moment more convenient. But we shall throughout be keeping in mind the extension of the argument to the explicit study of the demand for several commodities, which will follow in Part III. The particular form in which the two-good case is studied will often be chosen with the intention of making this later extension as easy and as general as possible.

PART II

THE DEMAND FOR A SINGLE COMMODITY

VI

THE DIRECT CONSISTENCY TEST

1. We are now to examine the behaviour of a consumer, who is confronted with a market in which the price of no more than one good is liable to change, so that he can (as explained)[1] be considered to be dividing his expenditure between two 'commodities'. Suppose that we have a record of his behaviour in various situations, which are such that the variable price does actually differ from situation to situation, while the income which he has available for spending may also differ from situation to situation. This is not, of course, in itself a very important case for study; but it is the right case for us to begin with, for there is no simpler case where theory has anything to contribute. It will therefore be useful if we explore it rather fully.

It is natural to begin by asking the question whether it is possible that this recorded behaviour could be the behaviour of an ideal consumer, who is 'revealing' an unchanged scale of preferences by the way in which he acts. Evidently we cannot hope to prove that the data can be explained in this way; other explanations which would account for them could always be invented. But we can hope to be able to show, on occasion, that an ideal consumer, who acts according to an unchanged scale of preferences, could not act as our actual consumer is found to act. The test which is available for this purpose has been made familiar to economists by the work of Samuelson; I shall here call it the Direct Consistency Test.

As before, we measure the commodity X (with variable price)

[1] See p. 37 above.

on the horizontal axis (Fig. 4), and the composite commodity M (which represents all other commodities) on the vertical. With given price of X, and given income, the opportunities open to the consumer are represented by points in or on a triangle such as aOa. The actual position selected in such a situation is represented by the point A, on aa. As we saw, the preference hypothesis (in its strong ordering form) implies that A is shown to be preferred to all other available positions *in* or *on* the triangle;

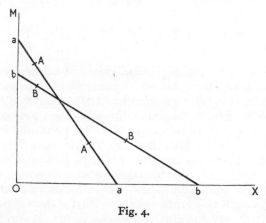

Fig. 4.

while if the hypothesis is taken in its weak form (with the additional hypothesis which then becomes called for) all that is implied is that A is preferred to positions within the triangle, and is either preferred or indifferent to other positions on the line aa.

Now consider a second market situation, in which the price of X is different, while the income of the consumer may or may not be different. The alternatives available in this second situation will be represented by points in or on another triangle, such as bOb, and that actually chosen will be represented by a point B on bb. Similar preferences are revealed in this case as in the A case.

If the consumer is acting according to the same scale of preference in both situations, the preferences which are revealed in the two situations must be consistent with one another. Since we are only comparing two situations, the only sort of consistency which is relevant is two-term consistency; transitivity cannot yet enter in. Let us consider what is implied by two-term consistency—the strong and weak ordering forms of the preference hypothesis being taken separately. For under strong ordering, inconsistency must mean that A is shown to be preferred to B in the A-situation, B to A in the B-situation; there is no other sort of inconsistency to be considered. Under weak ordering, we have also to consider the possibility of indifference.

2. Under strong ordering, the various cases that can arise can be classified in the following way.

It is possible, in the first place, that one of the two opportunity-lines lies wholly outside the other. (Let us say that it is aa which lies outside bb.) Then B must lie within the triangle aOa, and the consumer's behaviour in the first situation shows that he prefers A to B. In the second situation, A is not one of the available alternatives; the selection of B is therefore consistent with a preference for A. There can be no inconsistency here.

If the one opportunity-line does not lie wholly outside the other, the two must intersect. Let us suppose (for we have a choice in the matter of labelling) that aa is the one which lies outside the other on the left, so that it corresponds to a higher *income*, as shown in Fig. 4. There are then four main possibilities.

- (i) Both points, A and B, lie to the left of the cross. Then, as before, B is rejected in favour of A in the A-situation; but A is not available in the B-situation, so that the choice of B in the B-situation is not inconsistent with a preference for A.

- (ii) Both points lie to the right of the cross. A is now rejected in favour of B in the B-case, while B is not available in the A-case; behaviour is therefore consistent with a preference for B over A.

- (iii) The two points lie outside the cross, A to the left, B to the right of it. A is then out of reach in the B-case, B in the A-case. Nothing can be said about preference for one over the other.

- (iv) The two points lie inside the cross, B to the left, A to the right. If this happens, there is inconsistency. For B is now rejected in favour of A in the A-case, but A is rejected in favour of B in the B-case. Behaviour of this sort is inconsistent with conduct according to an unchanged scale of preferences.

Finally, we have a group of special cases, in which one point lies *at* the cross. If the other lies outside the cross, it is out of reach in one of the two situations, and no inconsistency can arise. But if the other lies inside the cross, there is inconsistency. For suppose that A lies at the cross, and B inside the cross. Then B is rejected in favour of A in the A-situation. In the B-situation, A costs as much as B does, but it is nevertheless rejected in favour of B. Under strong ordering, the B-situation reveals a preference for B over A, though the A-situation revealed a preference for A over B. Thus there is inconsistency.

If both A and B lie at the cross, the same position is taken up in both situations. Thus no preference is shown for one position over another, and (so far as we can see at present) there can be no inconsistency.

3. This is the strong ordering theory; does it make any difference if we make the assumption of weak ordering? There can evidently be no difference to the main possibilities; for if B lies *within* the A-triangle, it is shown under our weak ordering hypothesis, just as under strong ordering, that A is preferred to B. Thus (excepting in the special case when one of the points lies at the cross) there is inconsistency when both lie within the cross, but not otherwise.

Now suppose, as before, that A lies at the cross. Then, as before, if B lies outside the cross, B is not available in the A-situation, and there can be no inconsistency. But suppose that B lies inside the cross. Then B lies inside the A-triangle, so that (as before) it is shown in the A-situation that A is preferred to B. In the B-situation, it is not shown that B is preferred to A. But it is shown, even with weak ordering, when A is another point on the bb line, that either B is preferred to A, or B is indifferent to A; either of these alternatives is inconsistent with what has been shown in the A-situation. Thus the direct consistency test does after all appear to come out exactly the same, whether we are assuming strong or weak ordering. On either assumption, there is inconsistency:

(i) when both points A and B lie within the cross,

(ii) when one lies within, and the other at the cross

but not otherwise.

Though the two versions of the preference hypothesis give the same result, it must nevertheless be emphasized that the arguments by which they have attained that result are different. Thus we cannot be confident that we shall continue to find the same identity when we proceed to generalize. It is indeed quite easy to show, without embarking at this stage upon a formal statement of the general theory, that the complete identity ceases as soon as more than one price is allowed to vary. For this purpose it will be useful to make a slight digression into the analysis of choice among three 'commodities', which will help us to see the result just reached in better perspective.

If the consumer is choosing among three 'commodities' (X, Y, and M), the corresponding geometrical representation will require three dimensions, so as to give us three axes, along which the quantity of each commodity can be measured. With given income, and given prices, the opportunities open to the consumer will be limited by a *plane aaa*; the point A which is selected will be a point on this plane. If we are comparing (as before) two situations, we can continue to argue that it will be inconsistent with the preference hypothesis for B to lie within *aaa*, and A to lie within *bbb*; for the consumer will be showing in the first case that he prefers A to B, and in the second that he prefers B to A; he will be doing this whether we assume strong or weak ordering. It will further follow that if A lies on the intersection of the two planes, while B lies within *aaa*, there is inconsistency. All this is exactly the same as before.

Where there is a difference is in the special case where both A and B lie on the cross. In the two-good case, if both A and B lie at the cross, they must be identical with one another; accordingly no preference is shown, and there can be no inconsistency. But while two lines intersect in a point, two planes intersect in a line. Thus it is possible, in the three goods case, that both A and B lie on the cross, but that they are not identical with one another; they are different points on the line of intersection.

It is this possibility, and this alone, which gives different results according as we assume strong or weak ordering. Under strong ordering, the fact that A is chosen in the A-situation, while B is available, shows that A is preferred to B; the fact that B is chosen in the B-situation, while A is available, shows that B is preferred to A. Thus if both the selected positions lie on the line of intersection, and are different from one another, there is inconsistency. But under weak ordering, the selection of A, while B is available, only shows that B is *not* preferred to A; if B lies on *aaa*, this does not necessarily mean that A is preferred to B, for it is possible that A and B may be indifferent. The selection of B while A (another point on *bbb*) is available, similarly leaves it open that A and B are indifferent. Thus the choice of two different positions on the line of intersection does not involve inconsistency. What happens in such a case is that it is *shown* that A and B are indifferent.

4. Let us, however, return to the two-goods case, in which we do not have this complication, so that we have the same direct consistency test whether we are assuming strong or weak ordering. There is an obvious correspondence between this consistency test and the two-term consistency condition of the logical theory; the test is nothing else but the economic expression of two-term consistency. We have however learned, in our study of the logical theory, that two-term consistency is only one of the conditions which have to be satisfied in the composition of a completely ordered system; a further condition, transitivity, is always necessary. Thus if we had before us a set of data on the market behaviour of an individual consumer, it would not be sufficient, in the course of testing the preference hypothesis, to test for two-term consistency; we should test for transitivity also. There can be no doubt that, in general, a transitivity test is called for; and when we come to consider the general theory (in Part III) we shall have to set it out in a formal way. But this again is a matter where the two-good theory is simpler than the general theory; for in the two-goods case, the 'circular' ordering, which would be a mark of two-term consistency without transitivity, cannot arise—or rather, it cannot be 'shown' to arise.

If three positions A, B, and C were 'shown' to be circularly ordered, it would be necessary that A should be shown to be preferred to B, B to C, and C to A. Now if the two-term consistency tests are satisfied, this means that we have six conditions, which may be expressed on a diagram of the usual kind (Fig. 5). Consistent preference for *A* over *B* is shown (as before) when (i) *A* lies outside *bb* and (ii) *B* lies inside *aa*. Consistent preference for *B* over *C* is shown when (iii) *B* lies outside *cc*, (iv) *C* lies inside *bb*. Consistent preference for *C* over *A* is shown when (v) *C* lies outside *aa* and (vi) *A* lies inside *cc*. But all these things cannot happen.

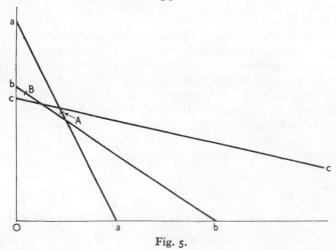

Fig. 5.

For the first two conditions show that *A*, *B* lie to the left of the *aa*, *bb* cross (as before). The third and sixth conditions then tell us that *cc* must pass outside *A* and inside *B*. (Since *cc* must be downward sloping, these conditions already set a restriction upon the possible positions of *A* and *B*.) So far the conditions are consistent; a line *cc* which satisfies them is shown in the figure. However *A* and *B* are placed, *cc* must intersect *aa* and *bb* to the left of their cross. There are therefore three parts of the line *cc* on which *C* may lie.

In the first place, it may lie to the left of *bb*. If so, condition (iv) is satisfied, but (v) is not satisfied. It may lie to the right of *aa*; if so, condition (v) is satisfied, but (iv) is not satisfied. Finally, it may lie between *aa* and *bb*; but if so, since it lies to the left of the *aa*, *bb* cross, neither (iv) nor (v) is satisfied. The satisfaction of all six conditions, which are needed to *show* circular ordering, is geometrically impossible.

We may therefore take it for granted that no additional test is needed, in the two-good case, to ensure transitivity;[1] though we shall have to look into the matter again when we come to the general theory, we do not need to concern ourselves with it farther here. The single direct test, as we have formulated it, being valid both for strong and for weak ordering, is the only consistency test which here arises.

5. But now, having got our consistency test, what do we do with it? It has been presented, as it is right for it to be presented, as a means whereby we could sometimes tell whether the behaviour of an actual consumer was or was not consistent with the assumption that he acted according to an unchanged scale of preferences. From the formal point of view, this is what it is. But is it really possible to use it, in the way it occurs in the

---

[1] Strictly speaking, we have not yet said enough to establish this result. We have shown that two-good data, which are two term consistent, cannot show three-term circularity; but the impossibility of three-term circularity is a consequence of transitivity, not the other way about. To have established that three-term circularity cannot be 'revealed' does not establish transitivity. It therefore remains possible that three-term circles are ruled out, but that more-term circles are not ruled out. The more complicated possibilities deserve, in strictness, to be separately checked.

In order to show that four-term circularity is ruled out we should have to proceed in the following way. We should study the possibility of a revealed preference for A over B, B over C, C over D, D over A, each with two-term consistency; while at the same time A and C on the one hand, and B and D on the other, were consistently related without revealing preference in either direction. (These latter conditions are necessary, for if A were shown to be preferred to C, A, B, C would be consistently related, but there would be *three-term* inconsistency in the A, C, D triad—and we have already shown that that cannot occur.) These conditions impose severe limits upon the positions which can be taken up on the diagram by cc and dd; it will be found that no points C and D on these lines can be found which will satisfy the other conditions.

This is sufficient to make one feel confident (though I do not have a general proof) that more-than-four-term circularity can be ruled out, in the two-goods case, in the same way.

(See P. K. Newman, 'The Foundations of Revealed Preference Theory', *Oxford Economic Papers*, June 1955. Though I had had the advantage of conversations with Mr. Newman, I had not read his article when I wrote these chapters. Mr. Newman gives, in his Appendix, an algebraical version of the above argument about three-term circularity. It is possible that the argument can be generalized by his method, though I do not myself see just how this is to be done.)

theory, as a direct check on actual material, such as that presented to us by the statisticians? There is a substantial reason why it is unlikely that we can in practice use it in that way.

The statistical information on consumers' behaviour, which is available to us, always relates to the behaviour of groups of individuals—such, for instance, as the consumers of a particular commodity in a particular region. It is always material of this

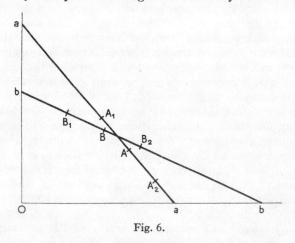

Fig. 6.

character which we have to test; and indeed it is material of this kind which we want to test, for the preference hypothesis only acquires a *prima facie* plausibility when it is applied to a statistical average. To assume that the representative consumer acts like an ideal consumer is a hypothesis worth testing; to assume that an actual person, the Mr. Brown or Mr. Jones who lives round the corner, does in fact act in such a way does not deserve a moment's consideration.

Now if the consistency test is applied to a group of consumers, it is necessary for the group to possess a most remarkable homogeneity if it is to give us a rigorous test of the preference hypothesis. If all the members of the group are economically identical, the test is valid; but if they are not identical, the test breaks down.

A simple way of showing this is illustrated in Fig. 6. Take the smallest possible group, that consisting of two individuals only. Assume, for the present, that the incomes of the two individuals are equal—that is to say, they have equal incomes in the first situation, and equal incomes in the second, though there may be a change in income from the first situation to the second. In the first (or A-) situation, each individual is accordingly confronted with the same opportunity-line aa; but unless the two individuals are exactly similar, the positions which they take up on that opportunity-line may be different. Suppose that the positions which they take up are A_1 and A_2. Now it is not very difficult to find a device by which we can represent the total consumption of the two individuals, considered as a group, on the same diagram. All that is necessary is that we should represent one unit of consumption by the group (of X or of M) by one-half the distance which was used to represent one unit of individual consumption. On this convention, the same aa line will represent the opportunities open to the pair taken together. The total quantities consumed by the pair will be shown as the *mean* between A_1 and A_2; total consumption will thus be represented by a point A, still on aa, but mid-way between A_1 and A_2.

Now suppose that the opportunity-line moves to the position bb. The first individual will now find A_1 out of reach, but he can *consistently* move to a position such as B_1. The second can consistently move to a position such as B_2. But if they move to the particular B_1 and B_2 shown on the diagram, the mean B (which represents the total quantities consumed by the group taken together) will lie inside the cross of the opportunity-lines; and this can happen even though A also lies within the cross. If the consistency test is applied to *group* consumption, it will appear to rule out positions such as this A and B; but it now appears that group consumptions of this sort can arise without implying any inconsistent behaviour on the part of either individual.

Now it will perhaps be objected against this demonstration that 'Apparent Inconsistency' (as we may call it) has occurred because of the differences in the preferences of our two individuals; and it is arguable that such differences ought to be excluded from the application of the preference hypothesis to group behaviour. It is the representative (or 'average') consumer whose behaviour is being tested, and in the case shown on the diagram he does *not* act as an ideal consumer should do. In this case the preference hypothesis, properly interpreted, *does* break down; the fact that its failure is due to heterogeneity of wants, and not to change of wants between one situation and the other, is immaterial.

It is undeniable that this contention possesses some force. But there is a further difficulty of the same character which has to be met, and which is harder to meet.

Suppose that our two individuals have the same wants, so that they would consume exactly the same quantities (of X and M) if their incomes were the same; but that in fact their incomes are different. It is still possible that Apparent Inconsistency may occur. In the first situation, suppose (as before) that the first individual takes up position A_1; then (in order to situate the choice of the second individual upon the same opportunity-line), suppose that the quantities which the second consumes are measured in units which bear the same proportion to those in which the first individual's consumption is measured as the one's income bears to the other's. The position taken up by the second individual will only appear the same as that taken up by the first (so that A_2 coincides with A_1) if each individual divides his expenditure between the two commodities in the same proportion. But even though their wants are the same, there is no reason why these proportions should be the same if incomes are different. In general, therefore, A_2 will be distinct from A_1. We can next, in the same way as before, show the group consumption on the same diagram by a further adjustment of units, so that A (the group consumption) appears as a *weighted* mean between A_1 and A_2—being nearer to that one of the pair which belongs to the individual with the larger income.

With this interpretation, the whole of the previous argument can be repeated. If the ratio between the incomes of the two individuals is the same in the B-situation as in the A-situation, B will divide B_1 and B_2 in the same proportion as A divided A_1 and A_2. But this still leaves it possible for A and B to lie within the cross, even though the behaviour of neither individual, in itself, shows any inconsistency.

It accordingly appears that if apparent inconsistency is to be ruled out, the group to which the test is applied must be homogenous, not only in wants, but also in income. We shall, I should suppose, rarely desire to assume such homogeneity. But if we do not assume it, the consistency test is not an infallible check. I feel obliged to conclude from this that there is in practice no direct test of the preference hypothesis.

We have, however, been by no means wasting our time. Though the argument of this chapter cannot fruitfully be used in the way we began by expecting to use it, it can be used in other ways. To the examination of these alternative applications we must now turn.

VII

THE DEMAND CURVE

1. Instead of dallying in the theory of consistency tests, an older writer on demand theory (one, that is, who was writing before Samuelson) would have proceeded at once, having laid his foundations, to the derivation of a much more famous principle—the principle that the demand curve for a commodity is downward sloping. We, in our turn, must now consider this basic proposition, which remains what it always was, the centre of the whole matter. Here at least there is no doubt about practical applicability, for on this principle all practical demand studies are founded. We can delay no longer in giving it our full attention.

The derivation of the law of demand is the first instance which we encounter of that technique of dividing the effects of a price-change into two parts ('income effect' and 'substitution effect') which was mentioned in Chapter II. The substitution effect is the effect of the change in price under consideration, combined with the effect of an appropriate change in income—which is chosen in such a manner that the effect of the combined change (the substitution effect) has definite properties that can be deduced from consistency theory. The income effect is the *remainder* of the actual change that has taken place. Since the change in prices has already been allowed for in the substitution effect, the income effect is limited to the effect of a change in income without change in prices. The consistency theory implies no particular rules about such income effects; but it so happens that there is a good deal of empirical evidence about the effects of 'pure' changes in income. It is this particular characteristic of the empirical evidence which is the justification of the whole approach. It follows that in strictness the law of demand is a hybrid; it has one leg resting on theory, and one on observation. But, in this particular instance, the double support happens to be quite exceptionally strong.

2. What we have now to consider is the effect of a change (say a fall) in the price of X without change in income—a movement which would be represented on the Paretian diagram (Fig. 7) in the following manner.[1] Since income is unchanged, and the price of M is unchanged, the amount of M which could be acquired, if no X was purchased, would be unchanged; thus the new opportunity-line (bb) will pass through the same point on the vertical (M) axis as aa. Since the price of X has fallen, bb will otherwise lie outside aa. It follows at once from the consis-

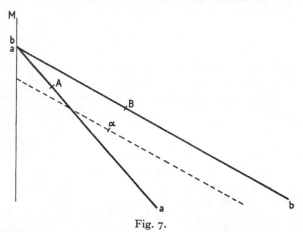

Fig. 7.

tency theory that, so long as some amount of X is being consumed in both situations, the position B (on bb) must be preferred to the position A (on aa). But this is *all* we learn from the consistency theory, when it is applied to these two positions. It is perfectly *consistent* for there to be a rise, or a fall, or no change, in the consumption of X between A and B.

It can however be shown, from the consistency theory, that if the fall in the price of X is accompanied by an appropriate fall in income, then the consumption of X must rise or remain

---

[1] As this diagram is ordinarily drawn, it shows the consumer spending a preposterously large proportion of his income on the commodity in question. This defect can be removed, without inconvenience in drawing, if we suppose the horizontal axis to be removed to a distance, so that the reader is left to imagine it to be somewhere at the bottom of the page. It is in fact only the top end of the diagram which we need; that is shown here, drawn on a large scale.

stationary; it cannot diminish. Thus it is possible to construct a position α, which is (in a certain sense) intermediate between A and B, and which is such that the consumption of X must 'tend to increase' between A and α; while the movement from α to B is the consequence of a pure change in income, an 'income effect'. (I propose, throughout this book, to use the term 'tend to increase' with the meaning 'increase, or possibly remain constant'; and 'tend to diminish' in the corresponding sense. This will make for brevity, and should not, in a static theory, cause any ambiguity.)

Since income is reduced between A and α, it must be raised between α and B. There is no theoretical rule which tells us that this rise in income must 'tend to increase' the consumption of X; but it is safe to conclude from the empirical evidence that it will do so in most cases, that the cases in which it does not do so may fairly be regarded as exceptional. Let us for the present set on one side these exceptional cases, in which the income-effect is negative (the cases of 'inferior goods'). In all other cases, we can say definitely that a fall in the price of X (income constant) must tend to increase the demand for X, by income effect and substitution effect together. This is the first thing which we have to prove.

3. In order to prove it, we have to make a suitable selection of an intermediate position. This may be done in two different ways, which give two alternative proofs. The first, which I shall call the method of the Compensating Variation, is that which I adopted in *Value and Capital*. The second, which I shall call the method of the Cost-Difference, has lately been advanced by Samuelson.[1] We shall find that each method has its merits, so that both require to be preserved.

According to the first method, we look for a position α which

[1] P. A. Samuelson, 'Consumption Theorems in terms of Over-Compensation rather than Indifference comparisons' (*Economica*, Feb. 1953). Samuelson's intermediate position has of course been used, in a vague way, for a long time; anyone who has tried to give an elementary lecture on income and substitution effects will have been almost bound to slip into it. But since the distinction between the two methods disappears in a mathematical analysis, based on calculus, it is only since the development of the new approach that it has been necessary to get it clear. To have shown that it is a distinct alternative to the indifference method is the latest of Samuelson's many contributions to demand theory.

will be taken up by the consumer, when the price of X has changed to the new figure, but when his income is reduced so far as to wipe out the gain in real income which he would otherwise get from the fall in price. Income is then said to be reduced by a *compensating variation*; the position α, taken up at the B price but with this lower income, is indifferent to A. This particular selection of the intermediate position α has the merit that the two parts into which the whole effect of the price-change is divided are parts that have special economic significance. For on this interpretation, the substitution effect measures the effect of the change in relative prices, with *real income constant*; the income effect measures the effect of the change in real income. Thus the analysis which is based upon the compensating variation is a resolution of the price-change into two fundamental economic 'directions'; we shall not encounter a more fundamental distinction upon any other route.

If an α can be selected by the method of the compensating variation, it is easy to show, from the consistency theory, that it has the properties that are required. Since the price of X is the same in the intermediate situation as in the B-situation, the opportunity-line upon which α lies must be parallel to bb (Fig. 7). Since A and α are indifferent, this line must intersect the line aa; for if it lay wholly outside aa, α would be shown to be preferred to A; and if it lay wholly inside aa, A would be shown to be preferred to α. The same reasoning shows that it is impossible for A and α to lie both to the left, or both to the right, of the cross of the lines on which they lie. If they both lay within the cross, or one at the cross and the other within the cross, there would be inconsistency. The only alternatives which remain are (i) that A and α both lie outside the cross, (ii) that one lies at the cross and the other outside the cross, (iii) that both lie at the cross. These are the only possible cases, if A and α are to be indifferent. In any of these cases, we can say (in our terminology) that the consumption of X tends to increase between A and α. Thus in all cases when X is not an inferior good, it will follow that the consumption of X must tend to increase between A and B.

So long as one assumes weak ordering (without which there can be no indifferent positions), this important argument

remains perfectly valid; and I shall have no hesitation in using
it extensively in the chapters which follow. But for the purpose
now in hand (the establishment of the Law of Demand) the alternative approach is somewhat more convenient. I shall therefore
proceed to examine the alternative method, that of the cost-
difference, postponing further consideration of the compensating
variation to the next chapter.

4. On the alternative method, we consider the effect of the

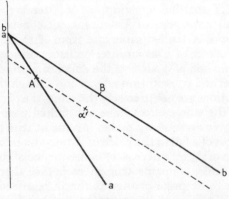

Fig. 8.

reduction in the price of X, when it is combined with a reduction in income which is such as will leave the consumer just able
to purchase the A collection of goods, if he so desires. Income is
accordingly reduced by the difference between the cost of his
previous (A) consumption of X, at the old price and at the new.
The intermediate opportunity-line will remain parallel to bb;
but instead of passing below A (as we have drawn it in Fig. 7),
it will pass, by definition, through A (as in Fig. 8). The new
intermediate position (α') is that which would be chosen by a
consumer, with the given wants, who was confronted with this
particular opportunity-line $A\alpha'$. It is easy to show that α', like
α, has the properties which are needed for the establishment of
our proposition, so that it can be used as a basis for an alternative proof.

Compare, in the light of the consistency theory, the situations in which A and α' are taken up. The two opportunity-lines are now aa and $A\alpha'$; one of the two positions (A) now lies *at* the cross of the two opportunity-lines, so that the list of possible cases is much reduced. For α' to lie to the left of A would infringe the consistency test; the only possibilities which remain open are (i) that α' lies to the right of A, (ii) that α' and A coincide. In either of these cases the consumption of X tends to increase between A and α'. It then follows, as before, in all cases where an increase in income tends to increase the consumption of X, that the consumption of X tends to increase as a result of a fall in the price of X with income constant, or that the consumption of X tends to increase from A to B.

Thus the choice of α' as an intermediate position provides an alternative method of analysing the effect of a price-change into income-effect and substitution effect; and though the two intermediate positions are not precisely the same, the parts into which they divide the whole effect have substantially similar properties. Whichever division we make, it remains true that the substitution effect of a fall in the price of X must tend to increase the consumption of X, by a necessary consequence of the preference hypothesis; and it remains true in each case that the income effect of the same price-change is the pure effect of a rise in income. The difference between the two methods is solely a matter of the magnitude of the rise in income, which leads to the income effect; and on this point the method of cost-difference has a distinct advantage. For while the magnitude of the compensating variation is quite a problem, as we shall see when we come to give it attention in the following chapter, the magnitude of the cost-difference raises no problem at all. It can be read off at once from the data of the situation under discussion.

5. If the consumer is initially spending no more than a small proportion of his income upon X, not even a large proportional fall in the price of X will produce a cost-difference which is more than a small proportion of his income. Then, unless the consumption of X is quite abnormally sensitive to changes to income (unless the income-elasticity of demand for X is abnormally high), the income-effect of the price-change must be quite small in relation to previous consumption. Suppose, for instance, that the consumer has been spending 5 per cent. of his income

on sugar (in practice this would be a distinctly large percentage);
and suppose that the price of sugar is halved. Then the cost-
difference, though half of his previous expenditure on sugar, is
no more than $2\frac{1}{2}$ per cent. of his income; the corresponding
income-effect is the effect on the demand for sugar of a rise in
income by $2\frac{1}{2}$ per cent. Now if the additional expenditure, made
possible by this increase in income, was divided among commodities in the same proportions as previous expenditure was
divided, a $2\frac{1}{2}$ per cent. rise in income would increase consumption of sugar by $2\frac{1}{2}$ per cent.; if it is to rise much more than this,
there must be a strong bias to spend an increment of income
upon sugar rather than upon other things. Thus, from this point
of view, 5 per cent. would be a large increase in consumption;
but if price falls by 50 per cent., and a large income-effect does
no more than increase consumption by 5 per cent., we are justified in saying that the income-effect is normally very small.

So long as the proportion of income initially spent upon X is
small, the income-effect is likely to be quite small. But there is
no reason why the same should hold for the corresponding substitution effect. Consider, for instance, the case in which no X at
all was purchased before the fall in price. The cost-difference is
then zero, and the corresponding income-effect must be zero.
But it is perfectly possible that the fall in price may have quite
a large effect in inducing the consumer to substitute X for other
commodities—the substitution effect may be very substantial
indeed. There is no reason why high elasticities of demand for
single commodities should not occur in appropriate conditions;
but they can only occur because of a large substitution effect.

In the ordinary, elementary, application of demand theory—
to the demand for a single commodity (in the ordinary sense) by
a consumer whose consumption is reasonably diversified—it is
fair to expect that the main effect of a price-change will be the
substitution effect, while the income effect will be relatively
small. The main exceptions to this rule will be in those cases
where the commodity under consideration is a theoretical construction—when we are considering the demand for a group of
goods, such as food, or clothing, or imports, taken as a whole.
The proportion of income spent upon a generalized commodity
of this sort will often be fairly high, while the opportunities for

substitution at the expense of other commodities may be rather restricted. Thus we must be prepared to find, in such cases as these, that the income-effect is relatively large. But full analysis of such cases will generally require the more elaborate methods which we shall be developing in Part III of this book.

6. As we have seen, it is by no means necessary that an increase in income should tend to increase the demand for every commodity in the consumer's budget; it is possible that there are some articles of which the consumption will diminish, for they are replaced by superior substitutes as income rises. The clearest example of this phenomenon occurs when the 'commodity' in question is an inferior quality of some physical commodity; it is for this reason that commodities with negative income-elasticity have been called *inferior goods*. But it is not inevitable that the inferior good and the superior substitute which replaces it should have any physical characteristics in common. It is not even necessary that the 'wants' which are satisfied by the two goods should be in any recognizable sense the same. Consider the case in which a person is induced, by a small rise in income, to run a car; he will then be obliged to economize on several of his previous lines of expenditure. For the particular rise in income which has taken place, all these ordinary forms of consumption will have become 'inferior goods'.

If X is an inferior good, the income-effect from a fall in the price of X will diminish the demand for X; but we shall still expect, for the reason set out in the previous paragraph, that in most ordinary cases this income-effect will be small. Though it now works in the opposite direction from the substitution effect, it is unlikely that it will outweigh the substitution effect. Though the law of demand does not necessarily hold in the case of inferior goods, it is in practice likely to hold. In order that there should be an exception to the rule that consumption tends to increase, when price falls and other things remain equal, three things are necessary

(i) the commodity must be an inferior good, with a negative income-elasticity of significant size,

(ii) the substitution effect must be small,

(iii) the proportion of income spent upon the inferior good must be large. It would be surprising to find that all these conditions were satisfied, in the case of any ordinary commodity. The second and third conditions may well be satisfied when we are dealing with a generalized commodity, which stands for a group of ordinary commodities; but the group of commodities will have to be selected in a very peculiar manner if it is to be inferior when taken as a whole. And it will indeed be remarkable if the group is easily substituted by goods outside it as a result of income-changes (negative income effect) but is not easily substitutable as a result of relative price-changes (low substitution effect). As soon as consumption is reasonably diversified, the Giffen case (which is what we are here considering) can hardly occur. Although exceptions to the law of demand are theoretically possible, the chance of their occurrence is in practice negligible.

7. So far we have been concerned with the reaction of the individual to price-changes; a word must be said, before concluding this chapter, about market demand, the demand of a group of consumers. The effect of a price-fall on the demand of the group is the sum of the effects on individuals; it can therefore be divided into a market income-effect (the sum of individual income-effects) and a market substitution-effect (the sum of individual substitution effects). Since each individual substitution effect tends to increase consumption, the market substitution effect must tend in the same direction. In order that the market income-effect should be negative (so that the commodity is an inferior good from the point of view of the whole body of consumers), there must be a balance of negative income-effects over positive, among the individuals. In order that the market income-effect should be strongly negative, it will probably be necessary that the commodity should be an inferior good for most of the individuals who have a substantial consumption of it; if this is not so, the negative income-effects of some individuals will be offset by positive effects of others. Now, in a heterogeneous group of individuals (with various tastes and various incomes) it is rather unlikely that the same commodity will be an inferior good for all alike; for the replacement of an inferior good by superior substitutes is not a thing which goes on all the way up the income-scale—it is a thing which happens, for any particular good, over a particular income-range. In a

heterogeneous group, there will be some people who are doing this particular replacement, but it is likely that there will be others who are not; a large negative income-effect is accordingly somewhat less likely in the case of a heterogeneous group than it is in the case of an individual. Cases do undoubtedly arise in which a commodity proves to be inferior for a large group of individuals; but a good many of the 'inferiorities' which might be expected to show themselves in analysis of individual behaviour will not show up in the behaviour of heterogeneous groups.

It will be remembered that when we were considering the consistency theory, we found that heterogeneity of a group made the consistency test less applicable. It is interesting to find that in the case of the law of demand, heterogeneity works the other way. The law does not work any less well when it is applied to a heterogeneous group than it does when applied to a single individual; if anything, it works rather better.

VIII

INDIFFERENCE AND THE COMPENSATING VARIATION

1. Since the law of demand has been so adequately established by the method of cost-difference, it might well be thought that the alternative method, that of the compensating variation, would not require any further attention. But we shall find that this is far from being the case. The merit of the cost-difference method is confined to the property of which we have been taking advantage—that its income-effect is peculiarly easy to handle. The compensating variation method does not share in this particular advantage; but it makes up for its clumsiness in relation to income effect by its convenience with relation to the substitution effect. The higher reaches of demand theory, with which we shall be concerned in Part III, are mainly concerned with further study of the substitution effect; thus they are for the most part more easily investigated by the method of the compensating variation than by its rival. In the simple one-commodity theory, with which we are concerned in the present part, analysis by compensating variation does not, it is true, have much more to offer us—apart, perhaps, from some clarifications of the concept of consumer's surplus, which have more relevance to 'welfare economics' than to demand theory proper. It will however be useful, as a matter of exposition, to set out the full theory of the compensating variation, in the first place, in terms of the one-commodity problem; though the matters which we shall discuss in this and in the following chapter are best regarded as being preparatory to the more general, and more constructive, treatment which will follow in Part III.

2. Before turning to the elaboration of the compensating variation method, it will be as well to consider its justification a little farther. We have already noticed that the use of this method is only justified if we can assume the existence of indifferent positions; and this at once implies that we are committed to weak ordering, for under strong ordering no indifferent positions will exist. But the weak ordering assumption, as such, is not sufficient to give us all that we require. For what we need is that there should be *some* income, which will enable the consumer, confronted by B-prices, to attain a position indifferent, but not superior to A. The weak ordering assumption, in itself, says no more than that some indifferent positions exist; this does not show that there is any indifferent position which satisfies our particular requirements. We have, however, discovered already that the general assumption of weak ordering requires a little modification before it can be used for any purpose of demand theory; we shall find that this modification (which we introduced in Chapter V) does in fact give us the assurance that we want.

If we assume, as we there found to be necessary, (i) that the generalized commodity M is available in amounts that are finely divisible, (ii) that the consumer will always prefer a greater quantity of M to a lesser, provided that his consumption of X remains unchanged; with these assumptions the existence of the required indifferent position follows at once. (No assumption about the divisibility of X is needed.) For we have only to consider the series of positions (B_1, B_2, B_3, . . .) which will be taken up at B-prices and various levels of income—positions which would be shown on the diagram (Figs. 7 or 8) by moving the bb line parallel to itself and observing the positions taken up. It is evident, first of all, that by increasing income sufficiently, we must ultimately reach a position which is preferred to A; without further refinement, this must happen when the bb line lies wholly outside the aa line. A sufficient reduction in income must, on the other hand, take the consumer to a position to which A is preferred; this must happen, again without looking farther, as soon as the bb line lies wholly within the aa line. It is therefore certain that there are some B-positions which are above A, and some which are below A, on the consumer's scale of preferences.

It further follows from our additional assumptions that a B-position with higher income is always preferred to one with lower income. For if income increases, while the price of X remains steady, it will always be possible to have more M and the same amount of X as before. This is a position which is established, by the additional assumptions, to be preferred over the position attained before income rose; the position which is actually taken up at the higher income must be preferred (or indifferent) to this, which means that it must be preferred over what was attainable at the lower income. Thus the various positions attainable at the B-price, at rising levels of income, are proved to be strongly ordered among themselves; successive rises in income must conduct the consumer to successively preferred positions. And we have seen that the whole sequence of these positions must conduct the consumer from positions inferior to A to positions which are preferred to A.

In this sequence, there will (or at least may) be positions which are neither shown to be preferred to A, nor is A shown to be preferred to them. But any such position must be orderable with respect to A (by the general hypothesis of weak ordering); either it is preferred to A, or it is indifferent to A, or A is preferred to it. Now if B_1 is preferred to A, and A is preferred to B_2, transitivity tells us that B_1 is preferred to B_2; and that means, as has just been shown, that it is attained at a higher income than that at which B_2 is attained. The B's attainable with income above a certain level are therefore proved to be preferred to A, while A is preferred to those attainable with incomes below this level. But what happens when income is precisely *at* the boundary?

At this point the additional assumptions come in again. For they assure us that there is an unbroken movement from positions which are below A on the scale of preference to positions which are above A; at the passage from one to the other a position which is indifferent to A must be found. We can therefore be certain that the position for which we are looking must exist; its existence is a necessary consequence of the fundamental assumptions of the weak theory. (See Note A, p. 195.)

3. Let us now proceed to examine what can be said about the *size* of the compensating variation. There is one rule about its size which has already appeared from Figs. 7 and 8, but we shall find that there is rather more that can be drawn out of this rule than appears from these diagrams. What we have already seen is that if the price of X falls, and income is reduced by the amount of the cost-difference, it is impossible that the best position which remains available (α' on Fig, 8) can be lower, on the

scale of preference, than (A) the position previously attained. For the previous position remains open in the new situation; if the consumer is unable to find any better position, he can stay where he was before. But the opportunities which are open to him in the new situation are different from those which were open in the old; thus it is possible that a position which is preferred to the old position may have come into reach. If the reduction in income is no more than the cost-difference, the consumer cannot be worse off, and may be better off, than he was previously.

It accordingly follows that the compensating variation, which is the reduction in income which just offsets the gain from the lower price, cannot be less, and may be greater, than the cost-difference. In our terminology, we may say that it 'tends to exceed' the cost-difference. But let us now turn to look at this upon a different kind of diagram.

We have so far been using Pareto-style diagrams, which are very convenient as a means of illustrating the foundations, and first steps, of the theory of demand. But as one goes on, they become less and less convenient. There is a reason for this, which is that the Pareto-type diagram gives equal emphasis to the commodity X, with the demand for which we are primarily concerned, and to the generalized commodity M, which serves as background. In the first stages of the theory, this is an advantage; but it becomes a nuisance as one goes on. From now on, we shall be much more concerned to concentrate attention upon the commodity X, the consequential effects on M being allowed to be covered by implication. From this standpoint, a Marshall-type diagram is much more handy.

Let us therefore proceed, in Marshall's manner (but without stepping, for the present, directly in Marshall's footsteps), to measure price of X along the vertical axis, and consumption of X along the horizontal (Fig. 9). We begin from a position in which the price is at OH, and the consumer (with a given income) purchases HA. We then suppose that the price is reduced to OK, while at the same time *income is reduced by* a compensating variation. As was proved in the last chapter, the consumption of X will then tend to increase. Let us represent this new level of consumption by Kb.

If we make *KN* equal to *HA*, and complete the rectangle *HANK*, the area of the rectangle will be a measure of the cost-difference which we have been discussing. What we have learned, so far, is the compensating variation tends to exceed the area of this rectangle *HANK*.

Now, making a further step, let us suppose that after being reduced to *OK*, the price is again raised to *OH*, with a *compensating increase in income*. The prices confronting the consumer

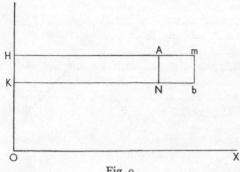

Fig. 9.

are now back where they were at the beginning, and he is in a position indifferent to that which he took up at the beginning; thus either he is back where he was to begin with, or he is in a position which he could equally well have taken up in the initial situation (remembering our assumption of weak ordering). In either case, his income must be the same as it was in the initial position. Thus the compensating increase in income, when price rises back from *OK* to *OH*, must be the same as the compensating reduction in income, when price falls from *OH* to *OK*. This must always be true, so long as the two positions are indifferent.

Now make *Hm* equal to *Kb*, and complete the rectangle *HmbK*. If, when price rose from *OK* to *OH*, income had been increased by the cost-difference *HmbK*, the consumer would still have been able to purchase the *b*-quantities of goods, though other alternatives would have been open, which were not open in the *b*-situation. Thus he could not be worse off, and might be better off, than he was at *b*. It follows, as before, that the compensating variation in income must tend to be less than the rectangle *HmbK*. We have accordingly got two limits for the compensating variation: it cannot be greater than the outer rectangle *HmbK* nor less than the inner rectangle *HANK*.

4. We can now proceed a stage farther. Instead of supposing that the price is reduced from *OH* to *OK* by a single step, suppose that it is reduced by a series of steps, giving a series of

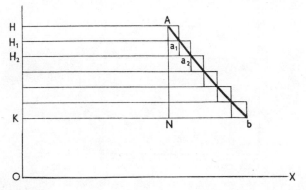

Fig. 10.

intermediate positions. At each step there is a compensating variation in income. When price is reduced to OH_1 (with compensating variation), there is, let us say, an expansion of consumption to H_1a_1 (Fig. 10); and when price is further reduced to OH_2, there is a further expansion of consumption to H_2a_2. It will follow, as before, that the compensating variation in income from *OH* to OH_1 lies between the inner and outer rectangles whose side is HH_1; and the compensating variation in income from OH_1 to OH_2 lies between the inner and outer rectangles whose side is H_1H_2.

It can further be shown that the compensating variation in income from *OH* to OH_2 is the sum of those form *OH* to OH_1 and from OH_1 to OH_2. This is a consequence of transitivity. For the change in price from *OH* to OH_1, together with its compensating variation in income, leads to a position a_1 which is indifferent to the initial position *A*; while the change in price from OH_1 to OH_2, together with its compensating variation in income, leads to a position a_2 which is indifferent to a_1. But if a_2 is indifferent to a_1, and a_1 to A, a_2 must be indifferent to A (by the transitivity of indifference). a_2 has been reached by a change in price from OH to OH_2, together with a change in income which is the sum of the two compensating variations. But since a_2 is indifferent to A, this change in income is the compensating variation from OH to OH_2.

We are accordingly enabled—in theory, but not, it must be admitted, in practice—to narrow the limits between which the compensating variation must lie. We can break up the whole movement from OH to OK into a series of steps, and regard the compensating variation from OH to OK as the sum of the compensating variations for the successive steps. The compensating variation for each step must lie between its own inner and outer rectangles; thus the compensating variation from OH to OK must lie between the sum of the inner rectangles and the sum of the outer rectangles (as shown on Fig. 10). The more steps we can interpose, the nearer these limits will get to one another.

Finally, if we suppose that price can vary continuously from OH to OK—and there is no reason why we should not assume this, once we have granted the divisibility of the background commodity—we can show a continuous expansion of consumption along the *curve Ab*, and the limits of both sums of rectangles become equal to the area $HAbK$, with the side Ab measured along the curve.[1]

5. This curve, which will play an important part in our subsequent analysis, is nearly related to the demand curve of Marshall. But it is not the same as Marshall's curve, which I take to be drawn up under the assumption that the consumer's income remains constant,[2] while ours is drawn up under the

[1] If the commodity X is only available in discrete units, there will be stretches over which the 'curve' Ab will be completely inelastic; and there will be certain prices at which the amount demanded will step to the right, a whole additional unit being taken in each case. The above argument in no way excludes the possibility of a 'stepped' demand curve of this type. The compensating variation will still be measured by a strip which is bounded (in the same way as shown) by this 'curve'.

[2] I am still inclined to risk the above statement, in spite of the ingenious efforts of Professor Milton Friedman to prove the contrary (see 'The Mar-

assumption that income is continuously adjusted so as to maintain indifference of the successive positions. There must clearly be a relation between our curve and the indifference curves of Pareto; but the relation is not quite as simple as might be expected, so we shall leave it over for examination on a later occasion.[1] For the present, we shall give to the curve Ab the name which is most obviously suggested by the approach we are making to it; we shall call it the 'compensated demand curve'.

The movement along the compensated demand curve measures the substitution effect of the fall in price; as we learned in the last chapter, this substitution effect is necessarily positive—the downward slope of the compensated demand curve is a necessary consequence of the preference hypothesis. The 'cost-difference', of our previous analysis, is measured by the rectangle $HANK$, while the compensating variation is measured by the strip $HAbK$; it is now geometrically obvious that the compensating variation tends to exceed the cost-difference, by an amount equal to the triangle ANb, the size of which depends, in its turn, upon the size of the substitution effect.

6. Though the compensated demand curve has to be distinguished from the demand curve of Marshall, there is no reason why we should not draw Marshall's *uncompensated* curve on the same diagram. If price falls from OH to OK, and there is no compensating variation in income, the consumer will have an additional amount of spending-power equal to the compensating variation; in the normal case, the consequential income-effect will increase his consumption, from Kb to (say) KB. The uncompensated demand curve AB will accordingly lie to the right of the compensated curve (as drawn in Fig. 11 *a*). But if the commodity is inferior, the income-effect will go in the opposite direction, and B will lie to the left of b (as in the second diagram of Fig. 11).

shallian Demand Curve' in his *Essays in Positive Economics*). Because of his assumption of a constant marginal utility of money, Marshall was at liberty to neglect the difference between the compensated and uncompensated curves; he does accordingly slip about, sometimes saying things which are appropriate to the one, sometimes things which are appropriate to the other. This, on his approach, was quite legitimate; but if he had wanted his readers to think *mainly* in terms of the compensated curve (which is a much more esoteric conception than the uncompensated) surely he would have said so.

[1] See below, Chapter IX.

Although the income-effect, shown in this diagram, is the consequence of an increase in income by the amount of the compensating variation, not of the cost-difference, we shall clearly be justified, whenever the cost-difference is small in relation to

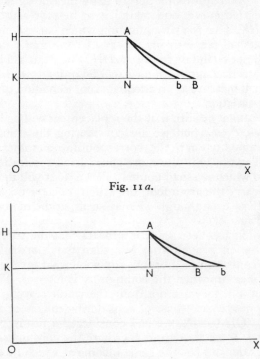

Fig. 11 *a*.

Fig. 11 *b*.

income, in regarding the income-effect as being small in relation to the substitution effect. For although the income-effect, as now defined, becomes somewhat larger when the substitution effect becomes larger, the increase in the income effect which is due (in this way) to the substitution effect must clearly be small in relation to the substitution effect itself.[1]

[1] Suppose, as in our earlier illustration, that the consumer is spending 5 per cent. of his income upon X; and that the price of X is halved. The cost-

In all such cases, B will lie very close to b, so that the compensated and uncompensated demand curves will lie very close together. Thus although the compensating variation should, in strictness, be measured along the compensated curve, we shall often get a good approximation to it by measuring it along the uncompensated curve, and taking it to be represented by the strip $HABK$. This is a simplification which corresponds to that which Marshall made in his theory of consumer's surplus, so that it will not be unfair to call $HABK$ the 'Marshall measure'. In many practical applications it will be quite legitimate to take the Marshall measure as an adequate representation of the compensating variation.

But we cannot be sure that the replacement will be legitimate in all cases, even when we are considering the demand for a single commodity; and the corresponding simplification will often be illegitimate in the more generalized applications of the analysis to which we shall come in Part III. It will therefore be useful to carry the argument, on which we have begun, somewhat farther—even though we may seem, at the moment, to be splitting hairs.

From what has been said, it appears that the true compensating variation is somewhat less than the Marshall measure when the commodity is normal, and somewhat greater than the Marshall measure when the commodity is inferior. These rules are correct, but they are not quite the whole story.

For suppose that instead of considering the effect of a fall in price from OH to OK, we had considered a rise in price from OK to OH. If we start from B (where the consumer is buying at a price OK, and has the same income at which he purchases HA at OH), our procedure will lead us to construct a compen-

difference is then, as we saw, some $2\frac{1}{2}$ per cent. of his income. Suppose that the substitution effect is fairly large, so that even when income is reduced by the compensating variation, the halving of price causes a threefold expansion of demand. The difference between the compensating variation and the cost-difference (the triangle ANb) must always be less than the substitution effect multiplied by the price-difference (the rectangle $ANbm$ shown in Fig. 9). Even when Kb is three times HA, this rectangle will still be no more than double the cost-difference, so that the compensating variation is less than $7\frac{1}{2}$ per cent. of income. It will still be safe to conclude that the income-effect, due to this compensating variation (considered as an income-change) will be small in relation to the rather large substitution effect which we have assumed.

sated demand curve, which will show the amounts purchased at
various prices, when income is increased at each price-rise so
as to compensate for the rise in price, leaving the consumer, at
each step, in a position which is indifferent to that which he

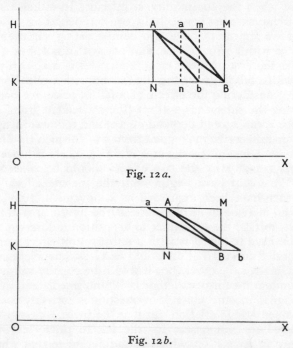

Fig. 12a.

Fig. 12b.

occupied at B. This compensated demand curve is shown as
Ba in Fig. 12.

When we compare the two compensated demand curves, Ab
and Ba, we observe that the consumer has a higher income at B
than at b, and at a than at A, with the same relation holding at
equal prices all the way up. In the normal case, a higher income
means a larger consumption of X, so that the Ba curve lies to
the right of the Ab curve; in the inferior case, it means a smaller
consumption, so that the Ba curve lies to the left of the Ab curve.
This, it will be noticed, is how they appear in the diagrams.

When we are considering a rise in price, the compensating

variation should apparently be measured along the *Ba* curve, so that it will be represented by the area of the strip *HaBK*. This, we now find, will be larger than the Marshall measure when the commodity is normal, and smaller than the Marshall measure when the commodity is inferior. In either case, the Marshall measure lies between the two compensating variations.

Thus we appear to have two compensating variations, one associated with a rise in price, and one with a fall; but it is not true that the first of these income-changes is necessarily associated with a fall in price, and the second with a rise. For when we were considering the effects of a fall in price, we began by examining the substitution effect (the movement from *A* to *b* along the compensated demand curve) and followed it up with the income effect (the movement from *b* to *B* which results from an increase in income by the area *HAbK*). There is however no necessary reason why the two effects should be taken in this order. We might have begun with the income effect, which would then have been expressed as a movement from *A* to *a* (due to an increase in income—measured by the area *HaBK*—sufficient to take the consumer to a position indifferent to *B*); and then have followed it with a substitution effect along the compensated curve *aB*. This would be a less convenient method of analysis than the other, but it would be equally valid.

If we adopt the former method (with intermediate position *b*), the change in income which is in question is correctly described as a compensating variation, for it is the income-change which is required to compensate for the fall in price, leaving the consumer in a position which is indifferent to that which he occupied originally. But if we adopt the latter method (with intermediate position *a*), the term compensating variation ceases to be appropriate. For the income-change which is now in question is that which would have an equivalent effect on real income to the fall in price—the change which, if experienced at price *OH*, would take the consumer to a position indifferent to that which he would be able to attain as a result of a fall in price (income constant) from *OH* to *OK*. I have therefore proposed[1] to call this latter change in income the *Equivalent Variation*.

[1] In 'The Four Consumer's Surpluses' (*Review of Economic Studies*, 1944), an article which included a first draft of the above argument.

In this terminology, which we shall henceforward follow, there is a compensating and an equivalent variation in income corresponding to any price-change. If we are considering a fall in price from OH to OK, the area $HAbK$ is the compensating variation, while $HaBK$ is the equivalent variation. But if we are considering a rise in price from OK to OH, the compensating and equivalent variations change places. $HaBK$ is then the compensating variation, while $HAbK$ is the equivalent. The distinction between the two variations is thus defined (as it has to be for the purpose of the generalization to which we shall be coming) with reference to the particular change in price which is taking place.

7. It will be convenient to conclude this chapter by giving a method of summarizing the results we have achieved, a method which will prove to be of considerable assistance in our further inquiries. For this purpose, we shall make the simplification of assuming that the compensated and uncompensated demand curves (Ab, AB, and aB) can be treated, to a sufficient approximation, as being straight lines (as they are drawn in Fig. 12). We shall further neglect the possible difference between the two substitution effects (Nb and aM) and in consequence that between the two income effects (bB and Aa). The compensated demand curves then become *parallel* straight lines. With these simplifications, the relations we have been discovering can be set out as follows.

Let us fix our attention on the case in which price is falling. Let us agree to reckon price in such a way that the fall in price (from OH to OK) is one unit. Then the substitution effect along the curve Ab can either be measured by the length of the line Nb, or by the area of the rectangle $ANbm$. Let us call the area of this rectangle S. The downward slope of the compensated demand curve ensures that $S \geqslant 0$. By our simplifications, the area $anBM$ is also equal to S. The triangle ANb is $\frac{1}{2}S$, and aBM is $\frac{1}{2}S$. The income effect is measured by the length of the line bB (or Aa); or by the corresponding rectangles. Let us call the income-effect (so measured) I; in the normal case I is positive, but it is negative if the commodity is inferior. The triangles AbB, ABa have an area of $\frac{1}{2}I$.

Let us denote the cost-difference of the initial quantity (the rectangle $HANK$) by L; that of the final quantities (the rectangle $HMBK$) by P. (These letters are chosen, for reasons which will become more apparent in Part III, by analogy with the forward and backward-weighted index-numbers of Laspeyre and Paasche.) Let C be the compensating variation, and E the equivalent. Let M be the Marshall measure. Then the following obvious relations may be read off from the diagram (Fig. 12):

$$P = L+S+I,$$
$$M = L+\tfrac{1}{2}(S+I) = P-\tfrac{1}{2}(S+I),$$
$$C = L+\tfrac{1}{2}S = M-\tfrac{1}{2}I = P-\tfrac{1}{2}S-I,$$
$$E = P-\tfrac{1}{2}S = M+\tfrac{1}{2}I = L+\tfrac{1}{2}S+I.$$

From these formulae, combined with the one necessary inequality $S \geqslant 0$, we get the following rules about the relations of the various quantities.

It is necessary that $C \geqslant L$, and $E \leqslant P$, in all cases.

If the commodity is normal, so that $I > 0$, then L, C, M, E, P are in ascending order.

If the commodity is slightly inferior, so that I is negative, but $I+\tfrac{1}{2}S$ is positive, C and E change places, so that the order becomes $L\,E\,M\,C\,P$.

These are the only cases which are likely to have practical significance, but there are two extreme cases which need to be added for completeness.

If $I+\tfrac{1}{2}S$ is negative, but $I+S$ is positive, C and E run outside L and P, so that the order becomes $E\,L\,M\,P\,C$.

If $I+S$ is negative (the Giffen case) L and P change places, so that the order is $E\,P\,M\,L\,C$.

All these rules have been set out for the case of a fall in price. If we want to apply them to a rise in price, the best way of doing so is to reckon the cost-differences, and the compensating and equivalent variations, as being negative. If we adopt this convention, the rules still hold. But this is a matter which may become clearer when we generalize this discussion in Part III.

IX

MARGINAL VALUATION

1. The demand curve of Marshall has two functions: on the one hand it shows the amounts which consumers will take at given prices, and on the other it shows the prices at which they will buy given quantities. When we are studying the behaviour of the individual consumer, it is natural to regard the former ('price into quantity') approach as primary, for the consumer is confronted with given prices on the market, and he chooses how much to purchase at a given price. But when we are studying market demand, the demand from the whole group of consumers of the commodity, the latter ('quantity into price') approach becomes at least as important. For we then very commonly begin with a given supply, and what we require to know is the price at which that given supply can be sold.

Now it is of course perfectly possible, when we have established the properties of the Marshallian demand curve by 'quantity into price' analysis, to use the results of that analysis for 'price into quantity' purposes. For it is the same demand curve which is being used in either sense. But something is sometimes to be gained by the adoption of a more direct method. As we shall find, it is possible to make an analysis of demand which proceeds throughout its whole course on 'quantity into price' lines.[1] Though, at the beginning, this alternative approach may appear a little awkward, it is not technically any more difficult than the other. And there are several ways in which it proves, when we have it, to deepen our understanding of the whole theory.

One of these ways may be mentioned without going farther. I have a strong feeling that one of the things which underlies the dispute between cardinalism and ordinalism, which we discussed in Chapter II, is nothing else than the distinction to

[1] Acknowledgement must be made to Professor René Roy for his systematic exploration of this approach. See his essay *De l'Utilité* (Paris, Hermann, 1942).

which we have now come. Ordinal utility theory, as hitherto set out, has almost always been 'price into quantity' theory; cardinal theory, in the hands of Marshall (or, indeed, of Sir Dennis Robertson), retains much more of the 'quantity into price' approach. But the latter approach, though natural to cardinalism, is not dependent upon cardinalism; by giving it the full weight which it can be given, even within an ordinal theory, we do in fact rescue a large part of the cargo which cardinalists have been accusing us of throwing overboard.

2. As has been said, it is at the outset that the 'quantity into price' approach runs into its difficulties. The alternative, which we have hitherto been following, started from the individual consumer, and built up its market demand curve from the demand curve of the individual. But how, on 'quantity into price' lines, are we to start from the individual? It is not possible to study the effect of an increase in market supply by allotting so much of the supply to each individual consumer, and then inquiring how much that consumer is prepared to pay for the given quantity. For the amount which is allotted to each consumer depends upon the amounts other consumers are prepared to pay; the price which is paid by one depends (under competitive conditions) upon the prices paid by others. Nor, even if we are prepared to treat the amount allotted to an individual consumer as given, will there then be any reason to suppose that the price which he will pay will be the same as that which would have made him willing to purchase exactly this particular quantity on a competitive market. If he is being allotted a fixed ration, there is no longer any competition; all that we can say is that there is a maximum price which he will be willing to give for the particular quantity; he may (and usually will) pay something less than this maximum price. It is very difficult to maintain the assumption of a competitive market on a 'quantity into price' approach.

It is, however, precisely this last consideration which gives us our clue. What, we have first to ask, is the maximum price which the consumer will be prepared to pay for a given quantity? Now this is something which already fits in with our previous discussion; it has been determined, in a wide variety of circumstances, by the compensated demand curve.

Suppose, as before, that the consumer has been purchasing an amount HA of the commodity at a price OH (Fig. 13). As before, if price drops to OK, and there is a compensating variation in income, he will purchase Kb. Now if we ask what is the maximum amount of money (or of the generalized commodity M, which—since its price is fixed in terms of money—may be taken, for present purposes, as being equivalent to money) which he will be prepared to give for the additional units of the com-

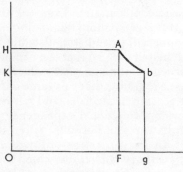

Fig. 13.

modity X, we can give an answer at once. We already know that the position at which he acquires Kb (or Og) units at a price OK, but at the same time loses an amount of money (or income) equal to the strip $HAbK$, is one which is indifferent to the initial position. Now this loss of money is equivalent to the payment of a higher price than OK for the intra-marginal units. He will be in exactly the same position as that which we have defined if, instead of paying a price OK and having the strip $HAbK$ taken from him in a lump sum, he pays OH (not OK) for the first OF units, together with a sum equal to the strip $AFgb$ for the additional units Fg. Thus we may say that, having purchased OF units at the price OH, he will be able to pay an amount of money equal to the strip $AFgb$ for the additional units Fg, whereupon he will finish up in a position which is indifferent to that which he initially occupied. Thus $AFgb$ measures the maximum amount of money which he will be willing to pay for the additional units Fg. If he pays more than this, he must end up

in a position which occupies a lower place upon his scale of preferences than that which he occupied initially; if he pays less
than this amount he gets a gain from the transaction—the gain
which Marshall called the Consumer's Surplus.

I propose to call the amount of money which is measured by
the strip *AFgb* the consumer's *valuation* of the extra units *Fg*.
But when we desire to bring out the analogy, or symmetry,
between this *valuation* and the compensating variation in income
HAbK, we shall allow ourselves to call it a *compensating valuation*. If the increase in consumption from *OF* to *Og* is small, so
that it may be reckoned as no more than a single (small) unit, the
valuation of that unit will be indistinguishable from the area of
the rectangle with height *AF*, so that the ordinates of the curve
Ab may be regarded as the *marginal valuations* of successive
units. Thus it seems to follow that this same curve *Ab* which we
have regarded as a compensated demand curve, when we considered it as showing a functional dependence of its horizontal
co-ordinate upon its vertical, becomes, when it is looked at in
the other way—with its vertical co-ordinate a function of its
horizontal—a *marginal valuation curve*, which shows the amounts
of money which the consumer is willing to pay for successive
units of the commodity *X*. But it is a marginal valuation curve
which is constructed according to a particular rule, which is
that the consumer pays the full marginal valuation of each unit
before making his valuation of the next. When we desire to
emphasize this characteristic, we shall call the curve a *compensated marginal valuation curve*.[1]

3. It does however turn out that the identity between the
marginal valuation curve, so defined, and the compensated demand curve of our previous discussion, though usually valid, is
not necessarily valid in all cases. No exception arises when the

---

[1] The curve might alternatively have been called a marginal indifference
curve, which is the name I gave to it when I first introduced it ('The Four
Consumer's Surpluses', *Review of Economic Studies*, 1944). For it bears the
same relation to the Paretian indifference curve as a curve of marginal product
bears to a curve of total product. In that article I used the term marginal
valuation curve for a curve which now seems to me to be of much less importance. I am now anxious to emphasize that all these curves are marginal
valuation curves, expressing the marginal valuation of the commodity as a
function of its quantity; I prefer to distinguish one from another by a qualify-
ing adjective, rather than by a distinct appellation.

commodity is only available in large units; each 'curve' will then descend in steps, but there is no sense to be given to a marginal valuation of anything less than a whole unit, so that the identity of the two 'curves' is unaffected. The exception which does need attention is of a different character.

Let us start from a point where the consumer has a given amount of money to spend, and (so far) none at all of the good X. Let us build up a (compensated) marginal valuation curve for X

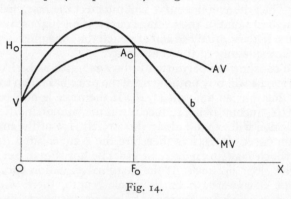

Fig. 14.

in its own way—asking, first of all, how much money the consumer would be prepared to give for a first unit of X; then, that amount having been paid for a first unit, how much would be paid for a second; and so on. There is no theoretical reason why such a curve should slope downwards from left to right over its whole course. There is no reason, for instance, why it should not behave as a *marginal product curve* is supposed to behave in production theory, having a first stretch in which it slopes upwards and only turning downwards later on (Fig. 14). But if this happens, the two curves will diverge; such behaviour as this is not inconsistent with the rule that the compensated demand curve must always slope downwards.

For consider the situation of a consumer, with a marginal valuation curve such as this, who is operating upon a market which is such that he has the liberty of buying any quantity that he chooses at a fixed price. Since his preferences remain unchanged throughout, and since he is to be thought of as paying his marginal valuation of each preceding unit before assessing his marginal valuation of the next unit, the total amount of money which he is prepared to pay for n units will be the sum of the marginal valuations of units 1 to n. The price per unit which he will be willing to pay for n units will be this sum divided by n. We can draw out this price in an *Average Valuation* curve, which has the same relation to the marginal valuation curve as average curves bear to marginal curves in production theory. Thus the average curve will intersect the marginal curve at the highest point of the average curve. This highest point A_0 shows the highest price *per unit* at which the consumer is willing to buy any quantity of the commodity.

If the consumer is permitted to buy as much as he likes at a fixed price, he will buy nothing until the price has fallen to OH_0; he will then buy an amount $H_0 A_0$. If the price is now reduced below OH_0, income being reduced so as to maintain indifference, consumption will expand along the stretch $A_0 b$ of the marginal valuation curve. $H_0 A_0 b$ is therefore the compensated demand curve, which may (in an extreme case) be horizontal, but which can never slope upwards. If the marginal valuation curve does not slope downwards over its whole length, there will be a stretch over which the marginal valuation curve and the compensated demand curve do not coincide.

There is therefore, in principle, an exact correspondence between the behaviour of the consumer under perfect competition and the behaviour of the firm under perfect competition. The firm's output is zero until price rises to its minimum average cost; the consumer's demand is zero until price falls to his maximum average valuation. Beyond that point, but only beyond that point, there is coincidence of the curves—marginal cost with the supply curve of the firm, marginal valuation with the (compensated) demand curve of the consumer. The two theories are in principle exactly parallel.

The importance of the qualification to the 'law of increasing marginal cost' is universally admitted; how important is the corresponding qualification in the case of marginal valuation? It must be freely admitted that it is of much less importance. But it is not difficult, when one looks for them, to find examples of the phenomenon. There are many articles which are worth little to the consumer if he can only have a small quantity, but which become proportionately more valuable (up to a point) when their quantity is increased. A gallon of petrol a year will run a petrol-lighter and take out a few stains; rather more will suffice for a lawn-mower; more again for a motor-bicycle. These cases of 'increasing marginal valuation' are not important in practice because consumers ordinarily operate upon what is to them a perfect market; but their unimportance is tied up with the perfection of the market, just as the importance of increasing returns in production is tied up with the imperfection of competition among producers.

So long as the consumer is operating upon a perfect market, the possible discrepancy between the two curves cannot cause any trouble. On a perfect market, it will be impossible for the consumer to demand any smaller quantity than that represented by OF_0 on the diagram; his behaviour will therefore be exactly the same as if a smaller quantity than OF_0 were not for sale. The maximum amount of money which he would be willing to pay for OF_0 units will be measured by the area OVA_0F_0 (taken along the marginal valuation curve); but this must, by definition, be the same as the rectangle $OH_0A_0F_0$ (which is the area under the compensated demand curve). We may therefore substitute the compensated demand curve, which can be relied upon to contain no upward-sloping stretches, for the marginal valuation curve, in any assessment of compensating valuation; in the technique of the theory possible upward-sloping stretches of the marginal valuation curve do not matter.

The fact that we do not need to assume that the marginal valuation curve always slopes downwards is however a point of some interest; for this marginal valuation curve is the nearest thing which we shall encounter to the marginal utility curve of Marshall. Marshallian economics began by assuming a 'law' of diminishing marginal utility; if we needed to begin by assuming a law of diminishing marginal valuation our approach would be in substance much nearer to Marshall's than it is. For, as it turns out, we do not need to assume the universality of diminishing marginal valuation; exceptions to that rule can be admitted within the present theory without any particular discomfort. The downward slope of the compensated demand curve, which is essential to our theory, does not have to be assumed; granted that we are dealing with a competitive market, it can be proved.

4. So far we have been concerned with compensated changes, changes which keep the consumer on the same indifference level; we can however go on to consider uncompensated changes in the same way. Let us begin from a position of equilibrium, in the usual sense, such that the consumer is buying a certain quantity of the commodity at a given price; the price is then, as we have seen, equal to his marginal valuation. Now let us suppose that the price is reduced, and let us consider the effect of the reduction upon the marginal valuations of extra units. If extra units had been offered to him, without any general reduction in price, at the maximum prices he was prepared to pay for them, their marginal valuations would be shown by the compensated curve we have been discussing; but that is not the situation which is here in question. Since there has been a reduction in the price per unit for any number of units, the amount of money which is left to the consumer, after he has purchased the old number of units, is increased by the amount which we have called the cost-difference; and this additional money may affect the marginal valuations of the various units of the commodity itself. The effect in question is evidently analogous to an income effect. Just as we had to make a distinction between substitution and income effects in 'price into quantity' theory, so there is a similar distinction in the theory of 'quantity into price'. There is a substitution effect *along* the compensated curve, and an income effect which arises when the change under consideration is not compensated.

What are the rules which govern this income effect? They are analogous to the rules which we got in the other theory, but they go *the other way*. The substitution effect, as we have seen, will ordinarily tend to make marginal valuation fall as quantity increases (subject to the exceptions which we have been discussing). The income effect will tend to raise the marginal valuation when the commodity is normal, but will lower it when the commodity is inferior. That this is so can readily be seen from Fig. 15.

In this diagram the price of X is taken to be reduced from OH to OK (without change in income) while consumption expands from OF to OG. Both A and B are equilibrium positions, with price equal to marginal valuation; AB is accordingly an uncompensated demand curve of the kind with which we are now familiar. The curve $Ab\beta$ is the compensated demand curve,

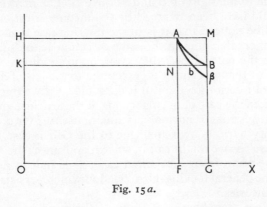

Fig. 15 a.

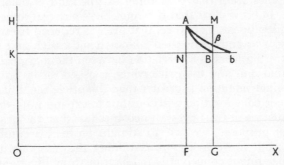

Fig. 15 b.

which we will assume to be the same, over that stretch, as the compensated marginal valuation curve through A. (That is to say, the possibility of rising stretches of the compensated curve is neglected.) Now if X is a normal commodity (Fig. 15a) the compensated curve lies to the left of the uncompensated demand curve, so that b is to the left of B, and β is accordingly *below* B. On our present approach, we proceed from A to B through β, not through B. Thus we think of the marginal valuation being reduced from AF to βG by the substitution effect, and then *raised* from βG to BG by the income effect. If X had been inferior (Fig. 15b), the reverse would have happened; b would have been to the right of B and β above B. The marginal valuation would have been reduced by the income effect.

It will be noticed that it is in the inferior case that we get an income effect that goes in the same direction as the substitution effect; in the normal case they go in opposite directions. Thus we now find that we can get no exception to the law of demand in the case of inferior goods. But it does look as if we might get an exception in the case of normal goods, if the article in question is sufficiently 'strongly normal'. Is this nonsense? Or does valuation theory have its own analogue to the Giffen case, an 'anti-Giffen case', as we might call it, since it appears at the other end of the spectrum from the Giffen case; as is indeed natural, in view of the general looking-glass relation which persists between the two theories?

5. It does seem that something of this kind is theoretically possible, but it is clear that it cannot be of any real importance. For let us suppose, as before, that price is reduced from OH to OK (Fig. 15); and let us then take each successive unit beyond OF, inquiring what is the relation between the marginal valuation of that unit and the price which is asked for it. So long as the marginal valuation is greater than the price, the unit will be purchased; consumption will continue to expand until the marginal valuation of the next unit becomes less than the price OK. For most purposes, we can go straight on to this equilibrium position; but if we insist on examining the previous units in detail, they might conceivably tell us something like the following story.

So far as the first unit beyond OF is concerned, its *compensated* valuation will be less than AF (assuming that the compensated curve is downward sloping in the ordinary manner). This, however, is the valuation which would be set upon it if it were offered in isolation from other units, the previous units being still acquired at the old price OH. Here we are supposing the price to be reduced to OK for any number of units, so that the OF units will have been acquired at a price OK. Accordingly (the commodity being normal) the marginal valuation of the first unit beyond OF will be put up by the income effect, so that it may well exceed AF, the *old* marginal valuation of the previous unit. This, indeed, is very likely to happen; there is nothing surprising or exceptional about it. But let us go on. If the first unit beyond OF is itself acquired at a price OK, there will be a big difference between its price and its marginal valuation; there is accordingly a further gain (a gain of consumer's surplus) which will induce a further income effect on the next unit. This is where the 'anti-Giffen' possibility may come in. It is conceivable (though we have no reason to suppose that it is likely) that this income effect might so raise the marginal valuation of the second unit as to make it larger than the marginal valuation of the first. This could happen, but even if it did happen it would not greatly signify. Though a similar increase might continue for a certain number of units, it could not continue indefinitely. Since the consumer's income is limited, his consumption of any particular commodity (at a positive price) must be limited also. Sooner or later the marginal valuations of successive units must turn downwards, so that *at the position of equilibrium* the marginal valuation of the quantity which is actually purchased must be equal to the price OK, which is (*ex hypothesi*) less than the marginal valuation AF (or OH) with which we began.

6. We may accordingly conclude that the 'anti-Giffen case' is of no real importance, just as the possibility of upward-sloping stretches of the compensated curve is of no real importance; neither of them could show up in actual market behaviour. As a theoretical possibility, the 'anti-Giffen case' is nevertheless of some interest; for one thing because of the light which it throws upon the Giffen case itself. Let us take the two *exceptions* and put them beside one another.

If we are merely studying the consumer's reaction to given price-changes, then we learn from the Giffen case that there is no necessity for a fall in price to be accompanied by a tendency to a rise in quantity demanded; it is conceivable that the reaction might be a fall in demand. But it is clear that if all consumers reacted in this exceptional manner, a market in which supply was fixed could not come to equilibrium. If supply was in excess of demand, price would fall; if this induced a *fall* in demand, there would then be a further fall in price. Equilibrium could not be reached until the zone was passed in which consumers acted in the 'Giffen' manner (or until the price fell to zero). If we neglect this last possibility, then we can say that the Giffen effect, in terms of market behaviour, would not show up. All that would be seen, when we compared one position of equilibrium with another, would be a fall in price, due to the excess supply, that was particularly heavy. We should not be able to tell that the law of demand was failing to operate, for the effects of that condition would be indistinguishable from the effects of a demand that was extremely inelastic.

Here, in valuation theory, we are supposing the price of the commodity to be independently given; and this has the same consequence as occurs when we take quantity to be given in the Giffen case. If, over a certain stretch, marginal valuation rose as consumption expanded, it would follow that over that stretch there could be no equilibrium. But in the end there must be equilibrium; so that all that would show would be a *strong* tendency for consumption to expand as price fell. Demand would appear to be extremely elastic. We should lose nothing in practical application if we gave this simpler interpretation to what we observed.

7. So far, the ideas which we have been developing in this chapter have led to quite negative results. They have perhaps thrown some further light upon foundations; but they have not done more than that. We shall however find in Part III that there are other applications which are much less sterile. And in the meantime they can be used for clarification of the controversial concept of consumer's surplus, which has already raised its head in this chapter, but deserves a more comprehensive discussion.

X

CONSUMER'S SURPLUS

1. Marshall defines consumer's surplus as 'the excess of the price which he (the consumer) would be willing to pay rather than go without the thing, over what he actually does pay'.[1] That is to say, in our terminology, it is the difference between the marginal valuation of a unit and the price which is actually paid for it. It is evident, from what has been said already, that the whole difficulty in the concept of consumer's surplus arises from the determination of the conditions under which this marginal valuation is to be reckoned. Marshall avoided this difficulty, since his assumption of a 'constant marginal utility of money' (his neglect of the income effect) enabled him to neglect the differences between the various marginal valuations which may be relevant. If we do not neglect these differences, Marshall's definition becomes inadequate. Various species of consumer's surplus then become distinguishable; it will be our business in this chapter to examine these species, and to discuss the relations of one to another.

2. We may begin by considering the *Increment of Consumer's Surplus* which accrues when the price of a commodity is reduced (income being unchanged) and consumption increases in consequence. This is the case which has already been exhibited in Fig. 15. The increment in question can be divided into two parts, one being the increment of surplus on those units which were being consumed previously (*OF*), the other being the new surplus arising from the increase in consumption (*FG*). The first part of the increment in consumer's surplus is simply equal to the cost-difference *HANK*; for here there is a change in what the consumer does pay but no relevant change in what he is willing to pay, so that all that has to be reckoned in the case of these units is the change in the price at which they are acquired. The second part is the difference between the marginal valuations of the extra units *FG* and the price which is paid for them.

[1] *Principles*, 8th ed., p. 124.

Thus if we reckon these marginal valuations along the compensated marginal valuation curve $Ab\beta$, the second part of the increment in surplus is the difference between the areas $AFG\beta$ and $NFGB$; which is the same as the difference between the triangles ANb and βBb. (This, it will be noticed, holds both in the normal case and in the case of an inferior good.) Taking the two parts together, the total increment comes out as the difference between the strip $HAbK$ and the little triangle βBb. It is this last which turns out to be the most convenient geometrical representation of the first of the magnitudes which we are proposing to study.

For the strip $HAbK$ is familiar to us as the *compensating variation in income*;[1] and our diagrams show that the increment of consumer's surplus (as at present measured) is always *less* than the compensating variation in income—by the little triangle βBb. If the income effect is neglected (in Marshall's manner), b and β will be indistinguishable from B, and the little triangle will disappear. The increment of consumer's surplus is then the same as the compensating variation. But in general there is this difference between them.[2]

What is the significance of this little triangle? The circumstances in which the consumer will move to the intermediate position we call b are those in which the price has fallen to OK, while he has lost an amount of money equal to the compensating variation in income; he can however purchase just as much as he

---

[1] We are here assuming (as we shall continue to assume throughout this chapter) that rising stretches of the marginal valuation curve can be neglected, so that the compensated marginal valuation curve and the compensated demand curve can be taken to be identical. For similar reasons, we shall neglect the 'queer' exceptions, Giffen and anti-Giffen cases. So long as we are comparing equilibrium positions, such neglect (as was shown in the last chapter) is perfectly justified.

[2] When I wrote *Value and Capital*, I was thinking entirely along the lines of what I here call 'price into quantity' theory; all my argument ran in terms of the effects of price-changes upon consumption, not in terms of the effects of quantity changes on marginal valuations. I accordingly identified consumer's surplus with the nearest thing to it which appears in price into quantity theory, which is the compensating variation in income. But this was a mistake, which was corrected in my article 'The Four Consumer's Surpluses' (*Review of Economic Studies*, 1944) and is corrected in the present chapter. But the credit for discovering it belongs to A. M. Henderson, 'Consumer's Surplus and the Compensating Variation in Income' (*Review of Economic Studies*, 1941).

likes at the price OK. In these circumstances he will purchase not KB but Kb. He is then in a position which is indifferent to that which he occupied originally. Now if, with price at OK, and income reduced by the compensating variation, he is nevertheless obliged to consume KB, not the Kb which he would have chosen, he will in general be worse off. (This is true whether KB is greater or less than Kb; for in the normal case, he is obliged to acquire units which have a marginal valuation less than OK, and in the inferior case, he is prevented from acquiring units with a marginal valuation greater than OK.) In either case, if he is obliged to consume OG, but is to remain on the same indifference level as at A or at b, the reduction in his income must tend to be less than it would be if he had a free choice of the quantity to be consumed. That is what we mean by saying that the increment of consumer's surplus tends to be less than the compensating variation.

3. This last interpretation—the reduction in income which would be necessary to restore the consumer to the same indifference level as before, while he continues to consume the same quantity of the commodity as he chose to consume under the more favourable conditions—seems to be the key meaning of the consumer's surplus concept which we are now studying. It is at once apparent, on this interpretation, that the increment of consumer's surplus, due to a fall in price, must always be positive. For if income is unchanged while the price of X falls, the new position which results must be preferred to the old position (so long as any X at all is consumed in either position). Some loss of income is accordingly necessary to preserve indifference. But it does not follow, as one might at first expect it to follow, that the increment of consumer's surplus is necessarily greater than the cost-difference $HANK$. It is true that if we look at the extra units FG in isolation, we can say that these would not be purchased unless the aggregate price paid for them was less than their aggregate marginal valuation; and it is tempting to conclude from this that the consumer's surplus *on these units* must be positive, so that the increment in surplus, as a whole, would have to be greater than the cost-difference in question. Yet this is not right. The marginal valuations which are shown by the curve $Ab\beta$ are those which *would* be set upon the corresponding units if they were acquired on such terms as to keep the consumer on the same indifference level as at A. In fact, he is not on the same indifference level as at A when he comes to buy these units. He has already made a gain to the extent of the cost-difference and it may be that he is only induced to purchase the extra units (or so many of them) through the income effect of this gain. In such a case (it does of course imply a rather large income effect) the increment in consumer's surplus would be less than the cost-difference $HANK$.

We know that the compensating variation in income is necessarily greater than the inner cost-difference $HANK$; but since the consumer's surplus is necessarily less than the compensating variation, it is not surprising that there should be no firm rule about the relation between the consumer's surplus and this cost-difference. But there is a rule about the consumer's surplus which corresponds to the rule about the compensating variation and the inner cost-difference. It is a rule about the consumer's surplus and the *outer* cost-difference (just where, it will be remembered, there was in the case of the compensating variation no firm rule to be found). The consumer's surplus is always *less* than the outer cost-difference by the area of the triangle $AM\beta$ (as may be confirmed on both diagrams of Fig. 15). The economic significance of this inequality is as follows.

Suppose that price has fallen to OK, and consumption expanded to OG, but that the consumer then loses an amount of money equal to the outer cost-difference $HMBK$. He then finds himself in identically the same position as if he had purchased OG of the commodity at a price OH throughout. But at the price OH, the amount of the commodity which he *chose* to purchase was OF; if he is obliged to purchase OG, he is in a position which was available but was rejected. Thus he is bound to be worse off (or, more strictly, cannot be better off) if he loses an amount of money equal to the outer cost-difference. The outer cost-difference sets an upper limit beyond which the consumer's surplus (in the sense so far used) cannot go.

4. So far, it will have become clear, we have been discussing the concept of consumer's surplus which corresponds to the compensating variation in income. There must however be another measure of consumer's surplus which corresponds to the equivalent variation—an increment of consumer's surplus which we may call the *equivalent*, while that which we have hitherto been discussing may be distinguished from it as the *compensating*. We reach this equivalent consumer's surplus by working with the compensated demand curve through B, instead of that through A. Suppose that this curve intersects HA at a and AF at α (Fig. 16). Then $HaBK$ is the equivalent variation in income. The equivalent consumer's surplus is the cost-difference on the units OF (as before) *plus* the difference between the aggregate price paid for the extra units FG and the *equivalent* valuation of those units. This latter difference is expressed by the triangle αNB (which is the difference between the price $NFGB$ and the valuation αFGB). Thus the equivalent consumer's surplus is equal to the rectangle $HANK$ plus the triangle αNB. As appears from both forms of Fig. 16, it is necessarily *greater* than the compensating variation in income by the area of the little triangle αAa; and it is necessarily *greater* than the inner cost-difference by the area of the triangle αNB. These are the two firm rules which operate in the case of the *equivalent* surplus; they correspond exactly to the rules which we have given for the case of the *compensating* surplus (as we have now decided to call it).

The economic significance of the equivalent surplus is quite straightforward. The compensating surplus measures the amount of money which the consumer would have to *lose*, after he had purchased OG units at the price OK, in order to find himself on the same indifference level as that which he attained when he purchased OF units at the price OH. The equivalent surplus measures the amount of money which he would have to *gain*, after acquiring OF units at the price OH, in order to find himself on the same indifference level as when he acquires OG units at price OK. The difference between either of the two variations in income (compensating or equivalent) and the corresponding consumer's surplus lies simply in this: that in the first case the consumer is allowed to adjust his consumption of the commodity X to the change in income which is imposed upon him, so that we consider his position after the adjustment has been made; while in the second case we suppose the change in income to occur after the quantity of X to be consumed has already been decided, and we consider his position before he

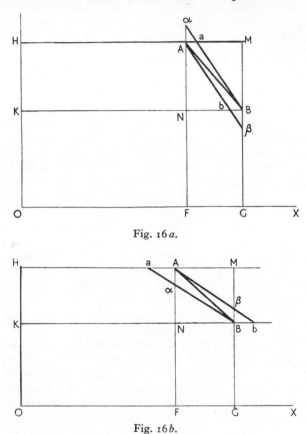

Fig. 16 a.

Fig. 16 b.

makes any further adjustment in consumptionas a r esult of the change in his income.

5. These are the main things that have to be said about the relations between the two income-variations and the corresponding consumer's surpluses; but there is one further proposition, of a more special character, which turns out to deserve a certain amount of attention.

It will be remembered that when we first examined the inequalities which govern the compensating and equivalent variations in income (Chapter VII above), we found it decidedly convenient to fix our attention upon the special case in which the two compensated demand curves were linear and parallel over the relevant range; not that this simplification would be generally valid, but that it would be approximately valid in most ordinary cases. When we did this, we were able to replace our inequalities by a standard set of equations, which were distinctly more manageable. So far, in this chapter, we have not needed to make any such simplifying assumption; but it is natural to ask if we should not get some interesting results if we made it here.

Let us therefore proceed to suppose that the compensated demand curves (or compensated marginal valuation curves) $Ab\beta$ and αaB are linear and parallel, so that they take the form in which they are drawn in Fig. 16. Since $Ab\beta$ is a straight line, the triangles ANb, βBb, become *similar triangles*; and we know from Euclid that the areas of similar triangles are in the ratio of the squares of their sides. But the ratio $bB:Nb$ is the ratio $I:S$; so that the ratio of the triangle βBb to the triangle ANb is as $I^2:S^2$. But the area of the triangle ANb is $\frac{1}{2}S$; so that the area of the triangle βbB (the 'little triangle' of our previous discussion) is $\frac{1}{2}I^2/S$. This vanishes, as it should do, when $I = 0$; it is always ≥ 0, whether I is positive or negative, since $S \geq 0$. The same formula will clearly hold (in view of the assumed parallelism) for the other 'little triangle' αAa.

With this little bit of assistance, the relation between the pairs of variations and surpluses can be expressed in the following sets of formulae, of which the first four are substantially the same as those which were given in Chapter VII. We use the same symbols as before: L, P are the inner and outer cost-differences; C, E are the compensating and equivalent variations in income; c, e are the compensating and equivalent surpluses. M (the Marshall measure) is the mean between L and P; in consequence of the parallelism which has been assumed, it is also the mean between each of the other pairs. Each of the other magnitudes may therefore most conveniently be written in terms of its relation to M. Accordingly

$$L = M - \tfrac{1}{2}I - \tfrac{1}{2}S, \qquad\qquad P = M + \tfrac{1}{2}I + \tfrac{1}{2}S,$$
$$C = M - \tfrac{1}{2}I, \qquad\qquad\qquad E = M + \tfrac{1}{2}I,$$
$$c = M - \tfrac{1}{2}I - \tfrac{1}{2}\frac{I^2}{S}, \qquad\qquad e = M + \tfrac{1}{2}I + \tfrac{1}{2}\frac{I^2}{S}.$$

Given that $S \geqslant o$, each of the pairs of inequalities which we have established is represented by these formulae.

(i) $C \geqslant L$, and $E \leqslant P$; for $C - L = P - E = \tfrac{1}{2}S$,

(ii) $c \leqslant C$, and $e \geqslant E$; for $C - c = e - E = \tfrac{1}{2}\dfrac{I^2}{S}$,

(iii) $c \leqslant P$, and $e \geqslant L$;

$$\text{for } P - c = e - L = \tfrac{1}{2}S + I + \tfrac{1}{2}\frac{I^2}{S} = \tfrac{1}{2}\frac{(I+S)^2}{S}.$$

Thus the formulae do sum up all the relations we have discovered.

6. Some of the lines of thought which are suggested by these formulae will have to be reserved for a later chapter; but in the meantime we may use them to give visual expression to the way in which the ordering of the variations and surpluses changes with changes in the magnitude of the income effect. For this purpose, we may suppose the size of the substitution effect (S) to be given; we can then plot out the variations and surpluses for different values of I. We need not consider values of I which are more negative than $-S$, for in the present analysis, the Giffen case makes no sense.[1] But we can let I vary from $-S$ to zero, and it can take positive values which are as large as we like, relatively to S. (Cases in which I appears large are to be envisaged as meaning that I is sizable, and S is very small.) Since M is the central value for each of the pairs, it will be convenient to draw the diagram in a form which shows the divergence from M as the vertical ordinate. This is how it is drawn out in Fig. 17.

It is evident that there are four phases to be distinguished. If I is positive and less than S, the consumer's surpluses lie between the cost-differences L and P, while the income-variations lie

[1] Cf. p. 96, note 1 above.

between the two surpluses. (This, we are probably right in supposing, is the 'ordinary' case.) If I is negative but small, between o and $-\frac{1}{2}S$, the consumer's surpluses lie within the income-variations, but these still lie within the cost-differences. But if the commodity is *very* inferior (I between $-\frac{1}{2}S$ and $-S$), while

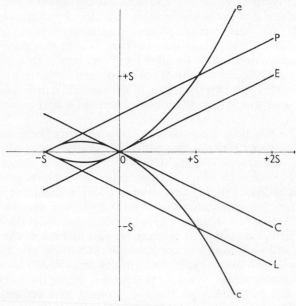

Fig. 17.

the consumer's surpluses remain enclosed within the cost-differences, the income-variations run outside. On the other hand, if I is positive and large (I greater than $+S$), the income-variations remain enclosed, but the consumer's surpluses run outside, and may run outside very far indeed.

All this fits in very well with what we learned in the last chapter about the looking-glass relationship between the 'price into quantity' theory of demand and the 'quantity into price' theory of valuation. So long as we are concerned with the effect of price on consumption, and with the compensating (or equivalent) variations in income which are associated with that effect, exceptional cases arise when the commodity under consideration is strongly inferior; so long as the income-effect is positive, we can rely upon the law of demand holding good without exception, and we can rely upon the income-variations falling between the cost-differences. But when we are concerned with the effects of quantity upon valuation, and with the consumer's surpluses which are related to these effects on valuation, inferiority creates no problems; it is in cases when the income-effect is strongly positive that queer things may happen. It is at this end of the scale that we find the anti-Giffen case; and it is at this end also that the consumer's surpluses may run outside the cost-differences, so that the two measures of consumer's surplus diverge widely, and the Marshall measure becomes a bad measure of either.

7. The practical sense of this last statement becomes very clear if we apply it to the case which Marshall so especially considered—the case in which the two positions under comparison are (1) a position in which the consumer is unable to purchase the commodity at all, (2) a position in which he acquires a definite quantity at a definite price. The first position may be taken as one in which the commodity is simply not on offer. So far as our particular consumer is concerned, his purchase of the commodity will be zero if it is not available, but it will also be zero if the price is higher than the maximum price which he would pay for any quantity. We may therefore consider the introduction of the commodity as being equivalent to a reduction in price, from an 'impossibly high' figure OH (Fig. 18) to an actual OK. All the magnitudes which we have been discussing can be interpreted in the light of this convention; but since the price OH may be *any* price which is high enough to make consumption zero, some of them will contain an arbitrary element.

It is interesting to see which of them are affected by this arbitrariness. The inner cost-difference is not; since the quantity initially consumed is zero, the inner cost-difference is zero, at whatever level the impossibly high price is set. But the outer cost-difference is clearly arbitrary, though it must be greater than the rectangle $AMBK$. The compensating variation in income is not arbitrary; it is represented by the triangle AKb, where Ab is the compensated demand curve through A. (A is now the point at which the Marshallian demand curve leaves the vertical axis.) The equivalent variation in income is quite arbitrary. But neither of the consumer's surpluses is arbitrary. The compensating surplus is measured by AKb minus $bB\beta$, as before; while the equivalent surplus is now measured by the

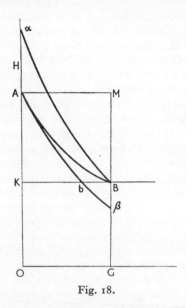

Fig. 18.

whole triangle αKB, where αB is the compensated demand curve (or marginal valuation curve) through B.

In any case where the income-effect is so small that the two compensated demand curves $A\beta$ and αB are almost coincident, the two surpluses will come together, and they will approximately coincide with the triangle AKB (Marshall's measure). But it is easy to think of cases in which the effect of the introduction (or withdrawal) of the commodity will be such as to make the two curves lie far apart. Suppose that we are dealing with an article which is such that, when it is available, it is regarded as a major necessity. Nevertheless, not very much of it may be demanded, so that when it is available at a moderate price, the proportion of income which is spent upon it may be small. If we put Marshall's question, and ask how much more the consumer would be prepared to pay rather than go without the thing, we get the compensating surplus. This may be very large relatively to his actual expenditure on the article, but there is a definite maximum to it—it cannot exceed the total amount which he has available for spending, less what he is actually spending on the article, or in other words, it cannot exceed the total of what he is spending on other things. But if we ask what we now see to be the corresponding question (which leads to the equivalent surplus) there is no such limit. If we start from the position in which he is able to purchase so much of the commodity as he chooses at a reasonable price, and then ask how much money (only available to be spent upon *other* commodities) he would require in order to be willing to give up the opportunity of acquiring the thing which he regards as a necessary, the position may be quite different. It is conceivable that there may be *no* conceivable compensation which would induce him to forego the form of consumption to which he is so attached. Even in the case of a necessary commodity, the compensating surplus is limited by income; but the equivalent surplus may be practically infinite.

I have a strong feeling that it was this paradox (as it appeared) which led several of Marshall's most eminent contemporaries to reject the concept of consumer's surplus. In the light of what has been said, I think we can now see where we stand about it. For any change in conditions which we may be studying, there are two surpluses to be considered, not one. But so long as the commodity in question is reasonably substitutable for others, and the income effect is small, the two surpluses will lie reasonably close together, and Marshall's measure will be a good approximation to either. It is when the article is not easily substitutable that the two surpluses may lie far apart, and Marshall's construction breaks down.

So far, we have confined our attention to the consumer's surplus on a single commodity (as we have been obliged to do by the general limitation of our approach in this Part). The question of the additivity of consumer's surpluses on different commodities will be considered in Chapter XVIII below.

PART III

THE GENERAL THEORY OF DEMAND

XI

CONSISTENCY TESTS

1. The effective limitation under which our analysis has been proceeding in Part II is that only such price-changes, among the commodities purchased by our consumer, were allowed to occur, as were capable of being reduced to changes in a single price-ratio. Granted this restriction, we could divide the whole set of commodities purchased into two groups (which we called X and Money), which were such that all price-ratios among the commodities included in X, and among the commodities included in money, were constant, with the result that X and money could be treated, for analytical purposes, as single commodities. Then the only price which is variable is the price of X in terms of money. The choice before the consumer is reduced to the choice between two commodities. It becomes sufficient to determine the demand for X at a given price; for once that is determined, the demand for the other commodity (money) follows as a matter of arithmetic.

The more general theory, to which we now come, is characterized by the assumption that more than one price-ratio is allowed to vary. It turns out that we derive no particular advantage from doing our generalization in stages—allowing two price-ratios to vary, and then more; it is just as simple to proceed at once to the general case. But we shall find that we derive great advantage from having set out the simpler theory in the particular form which we have given it in Part II, since we thereby find that we can avoid having to make any radically different approach to the general problem. We can repeat what is formally the same argument, step by step, and use it to develop much more far-reaching results. Many of these results are direct generalizations of those previously given, and we shall soon find that we can write them down with very little trouble. But from these generalizations there sometimes follow further propositions, which have no analogues in the theory of the demand for a single commodity. Most of our attention will have to be given, from now on, to these further developments.

Formally, we must now think of our consumer as dividing his expenditure among a number of commodities, X, Y, Z, . . ., the prices of which may vary in any manner. It will help us to think clearly about the more complicated relations which have now to be envisaged if we use a simple symbolism. We shall not need to manipulate these symbols; they will not be used to express anything which could not be expressed in words; but the symbolic statement will be a good deal briefer than a verbal statement. The quantities of the various commodities purchased by our consumer will accordingly be written q_x, q_y, q_z, . . .; but when, as will usually happen, it is the whole *set* of quantities consumed on which we are fixing our attention, we shall indicate the whole set by the symbol (q). The prices of the various commodities will be similarly written p_x, p_y, p_z, . . ., when we desire to discuss them separately; but when we are talking about the whole set of prices we shall write it (p). This device has the advantage that it leaves us at liberty, while avoiding a litter of suffixes, to use suffixes, as a general rule, to refer to *situations*. Thus (q_0) will indicate the set of quantities consumed in the first, or A-situation; (p_0) the prices offered in the A-situation. Similarly for (p_1) and (q_1).

We shall not usually need any special notation for income, because we assume that all income is spent, or that saving reckons among the set of acquired commodities. Thus A-income is equal to the total value of the (q_0) quantities at (p_0) prices. I propose to write this total value as $(p_0 . q_0)$. The total value of B-quantities at A-prices will similarly be written $(p_0 . q_1)$.

2. The well-known generalization of the consistency test of Chapter VI may now at once be written down. But, as before, we must be careful to distinguish between strong and weak ordering. If we take the preference hypothesis in its *strong* form, (q_0) will be shown to be preferred to (q_1) if (q_1) was available, but was rejected, in the A-situation. So long as (q_0) and (q_1) are

different, (q_1) will be one of these rejected possibilities if it is such that it could have been purchased in the A-situation; and the test for this is that the value of the (q_1) quantities at (p_0) prices must be less, or equal, to the income available in the A-situation. Thus if $(p_0 \cdot q_1) \leqslant (p_0 \cdot q_0)$, (q_0) is shown to be preferred to (q_1).

In the same way (q_1) will be shown to be preferred to (q_0), if (q_0) is one of the sets of quantities which were available, but rejected, in the B-situation; that is, if $(p_1 \cdot q_0) \leqslant (p_1 \cdot q_1)$. Thus the consistency test, in its most general form, says that it is impossible that

$$(p_0 \cdot q_1) \leqslant (p_0 \cdot q_0) \quad and \quad (p_1 \cdot q_0) \leqslant (p_1 \cdot q_1)$$

unless (q_0) and (q_1) are identical. This is the *strong* form of the consistency test.

Let us now ask what happens if we make the (economically more promising) *weak* assumption. As in Chapter VI, we need to make rather more than the unqualified assumption of weak ordering in order to get a usable result. It is necessary to assume that *at least one* of the commodities which are being purchased is finely divisible, and that the consumer will prefer a larger amount of this divisible commodity to a smaller, if the amounts of all other commodities are unchanged. Granted these additional assumptions, it follows from transitivity[1] that if $(p_0 \cdot q_1) < (p_0 \cdot q_0)$, (q_0) is shown to be preferred to (q_1); while if $(p_0 \cdot q_1) = (p_0 \cdot q_0)$, either (q_0) is preferred to (q_1), or they are indifferent. Thus it remains true under weak ordering that it is impossible that

$$(p_0 \cdot q_1) < (p_0 \cdot q_0) \quad and \quad (p_1 \cdot q_0) < (p_1 \cdot q_1),$$

and it is also impossible that

$$(p_0 \cdot q_1) < (p_0 \cdot q_0) \quad and \quad (p_1 \cdot q_0) = (p_1 \cdot q_1),$$

or that

$$(p_0 \cdot q_1) = (p_0 \cdot q_0) \quad and \quad (p_1 \cdot q_0) < (p_1 \cdot q_1).$$

What is not ruled out, in the weak theory, is that

$$(p_0 \cdot q_1) = (p_0 \cdot q_0) \qquad (p_1 \cdot q_0) = (p_1 \cdot q_1),$$

even though (q_0) and (q_1) are not identical. This is the sole difference between the consequences of the two assumptions, at this point.

[1] As on p. 43 above.

As we saw in Chapter VI, even this difference disappears in the two-commodity case; for it then follows from the double equality that (q_0) and (q_1) must be identical. But in the general case it does not follow. Thus the correct general statement of the consistency test, under weak ordering, is that it is impossible that

$$(p_0 \cdot q_1) \leqslant (p_0 \cdot q_0) \quad \text{and} \quad (p_1 \cdot q_0) \leqslant (p_1 \cdot q_1),$$

unless $\quad (p_0 \cdot q_1) = (p_0 \cdot q_0) \quad \text{and} \quad (p_1 \cdot q_0) = (p_1 \cdot q_1).$

This is the form in which we shall take the test to be expressed, from now on.

3. The test with which we have so far been concerned is the economic expression of two-term consistency; we must now proceed, as in Chapter V, to examine the economic expression of transitivity. We have seen that in the two-goods case, no further test is needed in order to rule out circular ordering; if the consumer's choice is limited to a choice between two 'commodities', it will follow, if (q_0) is shown to be (consistently) preferred to (q_1), and (q_1) to (q_2), that (q_2) cannot be consistently shown to be preferred to (q_0). It would be tempting to conclude from this that we need not worry our heads about transitivity and three-term consistency; but it emerges that three-term inconsistency is only ruled out in the two-goods case by the special properties of that case. Once we proceed to the general case, three-term consistency ceases to follow from two-term consistency. It would presumably be possible to illustrate this upon a 'three-dimensional diagram'; but such 'diagrams' are exceedingly clumsy, and for the purpose in hand such a demonstration is unnecessary. All we have to show is that it is *possible* for all two-term consistency tests to be satisfied, and for there yet to be three-term inconsistency. For so limited a purpose, one arithmetical example, which shows that the case in question *can* arise, is enough.

The following figures make no pretence to be realistic. Indeed they ought not to be realistic, for what we are seeking to identify is a case which (if the theory under consideration has any validity) cannot ordinarily occur. The point of the figures is to show that the rather absurd behaviour which they imply is not ruled out by the rules about two-term consistency.

Consider then the following sets of values for p's and q's, in which the numerical suffixes refer, as usual, to different price-situations:

Goods	p_0	p_1	p_2	q_0	q_1	q_2
x . . .	1	1	1	5	12	27
y . . .	1	1	2	19	12	11
z . . .	2	1	1	9	12	1

From these data we can construct a three-way table of $(p \cdot q)$'s, which comes out as follows:

$$(p_0 \cdot q_0) = 42, \qquad (p_1 \cdot q_0) = 33, \qquad (p_2 \cdot q_0) = 52,$$
$$(p_0 \cdot q_1) = 48, \qquad (p_1 \cdot q_1) = 36, \qquad (p_2 \cdot q_1) = 48,$$
$$(p_0 \cdot q_2) = 40, \qquad (p_1 \cdot q_2) = 39, \qquad (p_2 \cdot q_2) = 50.$$

Now, looking at the entries in the first and second row and column, it becomes clear from these figures that (q_1) is consistently preferred to (q_0); at the entries in the second and third row and column that (q_2) is consistently preferred to (q_1); but when we look at the entries in the first and third row and column it appears that (q_0) is consistently preferred to (q_2). Thus as soon as we have to deal with more than two goods, two-term consistency does not necessarily rule out three-term inconsistency; a special test is needed to exclude it.

Thus the consistency test which we have so far considered (the First Consistency Test, as we shall now call it) is not, in general, the only consistency test that can be applied to market behaviour. We should also apply a Second Consistency Test, in order to rule out three-term inconsistency. What is the precise form which this second consistency test ought to take?

It will, I think, be sufficient if we confine our attention to weak ordering. Under weak ordering, it will follow if

$$(p_0 \cdot q_1) \leqslant (p_0 \cdot q_0) \quad \text{and} \quad (p_1 \cdot q_2) \leqslant (p_1 \cdot q_1) \quad \text{and} \quad (p_2 \cdot q_0) \leqslant (p_2 \cdot q_2)$$

that (q_0) is preferred or indifferent to (q_1), (q_1) preferred or indifferent to (q_2), and (q_2) preferred or indifferent to (q_0). But the only condition in which all these statements can be simultaneously true is when the three sets (q_0), (q_1), and (q_2) are *all* indifferent. But if $(p_0 \cdot q_1) \leqslant (p_0 \cdot q_0)$, it is only possible for (q_0) and (q_1) to be indifferent if $(p_0 \cdot q_1) = (p_0 \cdot q_0)$. And similarly for the other pairs. Thus the second consistency test may be written, analogously with the first, in the form of saying that it is impossible that

$$(p_0 \cdot q_1) \leqslant (p_0 \cdot q_0) \text{ and } (p_1 \cdot q_2) \leqslant (p_1 \cdot q_1) \text{ and } (p_2 \cdot q_0) \leqslant (p_2 \cdot q_2)$$

unless all the inequalities become equalities, so that

$$(p_0 \cdot q_1) = (p_0 \cdot q_0) \text{ and } (p_1 \cdot q_2) = (p_1 \cdot q_1) \text{ and } (p_2 \cdot q_0) = (p_2 \cdot q_2)$$

4. Is this all? Or do we have to go on to Third, Fourth, . . . Consistency Tests between ever-increasing numbers of situations? It might be thought at first sight that since (as was shown in Chapter III) the one transitivity condition implies not only three-term, but also four-term, five-term, . . . consistency, higher-order tests would not be necessary. This, however, is not so. Though the preference system cannot be transitive unless the second consistency test is satisfied, the satisfaction of the second test does not prove transitivity. In principle, we ought to make all possible tests, up to an order corresponding to the number of observations.

All this becomes very complicated; but the reader will already be suspecting, in the light of what he has been told at the end of our earlier discussion of the consistency theory, that he is being led up a blind alley. We saw in Chapter VI that the first consistency test does not test the preference hypothesis if it can only be applied to the behaviour of a group of consumers; the same difficulty of compounding obviously persists in the case of the higher tests. It is useful to contemplate these tests, because they do constitute a part of the procedure which ought to be followed if it was desired to make a direct test of the preference hypothesis;[1] but we have already discovered (in our analysis of the two-goods case) that this direct approach is not promising. Just as in the two-goods theory, so now, we make better progress if we look for laws of demand than we do by the elaboration of consistency tests; the generalization of the law of demand is the subject to which we must now turn.

[1] It has been shown by H. S. Houthakker ('Revealed Preference and the Utility Function', *Economica*, 1950) that if a complete set of consistency tests is satisfied for all possible market situations within a given field, we can deduce transitivity and can therefore construct a complete system of ordering. This is a highly satisfactory conclusion to have attained; but the demonstration is very difficult, and it is fortunate that we do not need to make direct use of it in what follows.

XII

THE SUBSTITUTION EFFECT

1. Here also, as in the two-goods theory, the law of demand may be approached along either of two routes—by the method of cost-difference or by the method of compensating variation. In the two-goods theory, the method of cost-difference is perhaps preferable, though each has its advantages; here I am inclined to think that the balance of advantage lies on the other side. For we now have a longer chain of consequences to follow out; and most of the later links in that chain are unfolded more naturally if we use the compensating variation method. Though the cost-difference method must be recognized as perfectly valid, it will be more convenient to arrange our work on the other basis.

We are now to suppose that our consumer starts from an initial position A, in which he has a given income, and is able to purchase such quantities as he chooses of a set of commodities at fixed prices. Then prices change—in any manner—and, if we like, his income changes also; he proceeds to adjust his purchases and to acquire a different set of quantities which we may call B. What can be said about the relation between the A-quantities and the B-quantities? In order to answer this question by the method of compensating variation, we set up an intermediate position, in which prices have changed to their B-values, but in which income has changed in such a manner as to make the quantities selected in the intermediate position indifferent to those selected at A. The total movement from A to B is thus divided into (1) a substitution effect, being the movement from A to the intermediate position, (2) an income effect, being the movement from the initial position to B. This latter is solely the result of a change in income.

As before, it is not necessary for the validity of this analysis that we should be able in any practical case to identify the intermediate position; but it is essential that the intermediate position should exist. If we reconsider the arguments by which we established the existence of the intermediate position in the two-goods case, we find that they can in substance be repeated in the present connexion. The change to B-prices cannot make the consumer worse off than he was initially, if the income which he is given to spend at those prices is made sufficiently high; for a sufficiently high income will always make it possible for him to purchase the A-collection, if he chooses to do so, whatever B-prices may be. And the change to B-prices must make him worse off, if the income which he is given to spend at those prices is made sufficiently low; this is adequately shown by taking the extreme case of a zero income. Furthermore, if we grant the additional assumptions which are always necessary in the case of weak ordering, a rise in income (at B-prices) will always make it possible for the consumer to move to a preferred position, however small the rise in income may be; for he can always (at the worst) take more of the commodity which is assumed to be finely divisible. Thus, by changing income, we can move him continuously from a position to which A is preferred to one which is preferred to A; somewhere, on this path, he must reach a position which is indifferent to A. The difference between the income at which he reaches this indifferent position and the income which he had at A is the compensating variation.

2. Let us accordingly, at the next stage of our argument, examine the movement from a position (q_0) taken up at (p_0) prices, to (q_1) taken up at (p_1) prices, *when the change in income between the two positions is such as to maintain indifference.* We know, from the consistency theory, that if $(p_0 \cdot q_1) < (p_0 \cdot q_0)$, (q_0) would be shown to be preferred to (q_1); while if $(p_1 \cdot q_0) < (p_1 \cdot q_1)$, (q_1) would be shown to be preferred to (q_0). If (q_0) and (q_1) are indifferent, *neither* of these inequalities must hold. Thus if (q_0) and (q_1) are indifferent, it follows that

$$(p_0 \cdot q_1) \geqslant (p_0 \cdot q_0) \quad \text{and} \quad (p_1 \cdot q_0) \geqslant (p_1 \cdot q_1).$$

(The case in which *both* inequalities become equalities *is* admitted, even though (q_0) and (q_1) are not identical, because we are now firmly committed to a *weak* theory.)

It will be useful to have a name for these inequalities; we shall call them the Indifference Tests. There is an obvious symmetry between the indifference tests and the two parts of the first consistency test, which are exactly the same with signs reversed. But whereas the first consistency test says that both its two conditions must *not* be satisfied, both of the two indifference tests *must* be satisfied. Thus the indifference tests are two tests, while the first consistency test is only one. Two tests tell us more than one, and have the further advantage that they can be combined arithmetically to give further results.

There are doubtless several possible ways of combining them, but there are two which appear to be basic. Only the first of these will be explained in this chapter; we shall find that it opens up a line of analysis which will occupy us for most of the rest of this book. But there is another distinct combination, which would conduct us in a totally different direction. I shall be returning to that other combination in Chapter XIX—on the 'Index Number theorem'.

3. In order to make the first combination in the most significant manner, we may begin by writing the indifference tests in another way. Suppose, to begin with, that the change in prices from (p_0) to (p_1) is on the whole favourable to our consumer, so that in order to maintain indifference, his income must be *reduced*. We should then write the compensating variation in income as

$$(p_0 \cdot q_0) - (p_1 \cdot q_1).$$

If, on the other hand, we were dealing with a price-change that was on the whole unfavourable, income would have to be raised, and it might seem natural to write the compensating variation the other way about. We shall, however, get into trouble if we do not agree upon a single formula for the compensating variation. I shall adopt the convention of always reckoning the compensating variation in income (between indifferent positions) as

$$(p_0 \cdot q_0) - (p_1 \cdot q_1),$$

which means that for an unfavourable change in prices the compensating variation is *negative*.

Now if we subtract $(p_1 \cdot q_1)$ from each of the sums in the first of the indifference tests, we get

$$(p_0 \cdot q_1) - (p_1 \cdot q_1) \geqslant (p_0 \cdot q_0) - (p_1 \cdot q_1).$$

The second of these differences is the compensating variation; while the first—which might alternatively be written $(p_0 - p_1 . q_1)$ —is the cost-difference of the (q_1) quantities. This cost-difference corresponds exactly to what we called in Part II the 'outer' or 'Paasche' cost-difference—the cost-difference which we labelled P. Thus the *first* of the indifference tests reduces to the statement that as between two indifferent positions, the compensating variation C is less or equal to the cost-difference P.

If we similarly subtract $(p_0 . q_0)$ from each of the sums in the second indifference test, it reduces to the statement that $-L \geqslant -C$, where L is the 'inner' or 'Laspeyre' cost-difference. But if $-L \geqslant -C$, $C \geqslant L$. Thus the second indifference test is expressed by saying that when we are comparing two indifferent positions, C must be greater or equal to L.

These interpretations of the indifference tests are, it should be observed, quite generally valid. In the case when the change in prices is favourable to the consumer, L, C, P will usually be all of them positive, and we have now learned that they are in ascending order. In the case where they are all negative, the same inequalities hold. But now, if $L \leqslant C \leqslant P$, it follows that $-L \geqslant -C \geqslant -P$, so that when all three are negative, the compensating variation is greater in *size* than the Paasche cost-difference, and smaller in *size* than the Laspeyre cost-difference. This is, of course, as it should be; for if we begin by considering a movement when the change in *prices* is favourable to the consumer, and then look at the same movement in reverse, the Laspeyre cost-difference of the one becomes the Paasche cost-difference of the other (with sign changed). By adopting the convention of a change in sign to mark change in direction we are enabled to keep $L \leqslant C \leqslant P$ throughout.

3. We have now got ourselves on to a route where the stations are readily recognizable. As between two indifferent positions, $L \leqslant C \leqslant P$; consequently $L \leqslant P$. If, as in Chapter VII, we write $P - L = S$ (for since we are now comparing indifferent positions, $I = 0$), we learn from the indifference tests that $S \geqslant 0$. As in the two-goods theory, S may be regarded as a measure of the substitution effect of the price-change. In the two-goods theory, $S \geqslant 0$ symbolized the downward slope of the compensated demand curve. What does it signify here?

We have

$$S = P - L = (p_0 - p_1 \cdot q_1) - (p_0 - p_1 \cdot q_0) = (p_0 - p_1 \cdot q_1 - q_0).$$

This is the sum-product of the differences in price (falls in price being reckoned as positive) and the differences in quantity consumed (rises in quantity being reckoned as positive). Alternatively, it is the sum (with proper attention to sign) of the differences in quantity consumed of each good, each being valued at the corresponding difference in price. This sum may very naturally be regarded as the Total Substitution Effect of the price-change. Thus what we learn, as a first corollary of the indifference tests, is that the total substitution effect of any price-change, however complex, always *tends* to be positive. It will be convenient to have a name for this important principle. Though we shall subsequently meet it in other guises, I propose to call it, for the present, the First Substitution Theorem.

In order to show precisely what is implied in this theorem, we may proceed to take a number of relatively simple examples. In the first place, if only one price (that of the commodity X) is changing, the difference $p_0 - p_1$ will vanish for all commodities other than X. The product $p_0 - p_1 \cdot q_1 - q_0$ will therefore vanish for all commodities other than X. The sum-product S accordingly reduces to the simple product $(p_0 - p_1)(q_1 - q_0)$ in which all p's and q's refer to the commodity X. Thus if $S \geqslant 0$, it follows that both differences must be positive, or both negative (unless one is zero). A fall in price tends to be accompanied by a rise in quantity; a rise in price by a fall in quantity. In other words, the first substitution theorem contains, as it should, the downward slope of the compensated demand curve as a special case.

Suppose, secondly, that there are changes in the prices of two commodities, X and Y. There are now two terms in the sum-product S (all the others dropping out as before), which may be written in full

$$(p_{0x} - p_{1x})(q_{1x} - q_{0x}) + (p_{0y} - p_{1y})(q_{1y} - q_{0y}).$$

Now this expression will be positive (or zero) if both of the two terms which compose it are positive (or zero); but it is possible that $S \geqslant 0$ even if *one* of the two terms is negative, provided that its negativeness is counterbalanced by positiveness of the other. Thus if there is a double price-fall (a fall in the prices of X

and of Y), it may lead to an expansion in the consumption of both X and Y, but it is not necessary that it should do so. It is quite possible that the consumption of one of the two commodities may contract, provided that the contraction is counterbalanced by expansion in the consumption of the other commodity. It is not possible for the consumption of both commodities to contract as the result of a double (compensated) fall in price.

The case of a double rise in price is obviously similar; but it is worth noticing that we get similar rules for the case of a mixed change, when the prices of X and Y move in opposite directions. (In this case it is quite possible that L and P may have opposite signs, and it is very possible, if so, that the compensating variation may be negligible.) If two prices vary, one falling and the other rising, it is possible that both demands may rise, or both fall; what is not possible is that the demands for both commodities should move in the 'wrong' direction. The extent of the double fall (or rise) that is possible is again limited by the formula.

4. In the general case, when many prices vary, the first substitution theorem may be interpreted as indicating a sense in which prices and quantities must move, on the whole, in opposite directions. The sense in question is clearly related to the statistical notion of negative correlation; but its significance, in a more narrowly economic sense, may be illustrated, before going farther, by the following special example. Though this illustration takes us a little outside the field in which we have been working, it may be useful as an indication of the close relevance of our discussion to the central issues of economic theory.

Suppose that a particular factor of production F is being used in the manufacture of a number of commodities; and that a fixed amount of the factor per unit of product is required in each 'industry'. (Compare the *fixed technical coefficients* of Walras and Leontief.) Let $f_x, f_y, f_z, \ldots$ be the quantities of F used for the production of a unit of $X, Y, Z, \ldots$ respectively; so that the *set* of technical coefficients may be written (f), in accordance with our usual practice. Suppose that the prices of the commodities are fixed in such a way as to equal their costs of production.

Then, when the price of the factor F falls from π_0 to π_1, the prices of the commodities will fall in such a way as to make, for each commodity $p_0 - p_1 = (\pi_0 - \pi_1)f$.

Now the first substitution theorem tells us that, for a consumer who suffers a compensating variation in income,

$$S = (p_0 - p_1 \cdot q_1 - q_0) \geqslant 0.$$

But the difference in the price of the factor (per unit of factor) is the same in all industries; S may accordingly be rewritten

$$(\pi_0 - \pi_1)(f \cdot q_1 - q_0).$$

But the sum-product $(f.q)$ is the quantity of the factor F which is needed to produce the set of quantities of commodities which we have called (q); thus $(f.q_1 - q_0)$ measures the change in the demand for the factor F. Thus S reduces to a single term, which is the product of the difference in the price of the factor and the difference in the total quantity of the factor required. What the first substitution theorem tells us is that the derived demand for the factor, from a consumer who suffers a compensating variation in income, will always tend to increase when the price of the factor falls. Although it is quite possible that the demands for some particular products may contract in the course of adjustment to a multiple fall in commodity prices, these abnormal movements cannot go so far as to prevent a general tendency to expansion of the derived demand for the factor of production by whose fall in price the whole process was set off.

In such applications as this, the first substitution theorem already takes us a long way. But we shall now proceed to show that this Theorem is not the only thing which can be extracted from close study of the indifference tests, even while we keep to the same basic route.

XIII

THE RECIPROCITY THEOREM

1. This is the point, in the general theory of demand, at which we have to make our most important use of the transitivity assumption. It is, I think, unnecessary to argue the case for the legitimacy of that assumption all over again. We have been unable to get even as far as this without making some use of transitivity. There is therefore no reason why we should not use it farther.

Since we are still comparing indifferent positions, the particular form of transitivity which we now need to invoke is the transitivity of indifference. If A is indifferent to B, and B to C, A must be indifferent to C. From this seemingly obvious principle there follows another, which is quite important, and much less obvious—the *additivity* of compensating variations.

If prices change from (p_0) to (p_1), and there is a compensating variation in income, the consumptions (q_0) and (q_1) will be indifferent. If prices then change from (p_1) to (p_2), and there is a compensating variation in income, (q_1) and (q_2) will be indifferent. Therefore, by the transitivity of indifference, (q_0) and (q_2) will be indifferent. But the change in income from (q_0) to (q_2) is the sum of the compensating variations from (q_0) to (q_1) and from (q_1) to (q_2). And this has been shown to conduct the consumer to an indifferent position. Thus the compensating variation from (p_0) to (p_2) is the sum of the compensating variations from (p_0) to (p_1) and from (p_1) to (p_2).

The additivity of compensating variations once established, we can imitate the argument which we used in Part II to narrow the gap between the Laspeyre and Paasche limits between which any compensating variation must lie. In the form which we there gave to it, it depended rather heavily upon the geometrical properties of the demand curve diagram. The general additivity principle, which we have just established, now stands in the place of those geometrical properties. It will, however, be convenient, as a matter of exposition, to use a 'ghost' of the demand curve diagram which can still be applied here, and which is constructed in the following way.

2. Let us begin, for simplicity, with the case in which prices 'on the whole' are falling from (p_0) to (p_1); or, more precisely, when the change is such that the Laspeyre cost-difference $(p_0 - p_1 . q_0)$ is positive. Then, by the substitution theorem between indifferent positions, the Paasche cost-difference $(p_0 - p_1 . q_1)$ must also be positive. Set up a vertical axis (Fig. 19) and mark

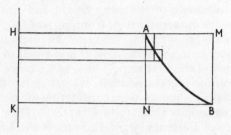

Fig. 19.

an *arbitrary* length, HK, upon it. On this construct two rectangles $HANK$, $HMBK$, the *areas* of which represent the Laspeyre and Paasche cost-differences respectively. What we have learned so far is that B tends to lie to the right of A, and that the compensating variation lies between the two rectangles.

Now suppose that the price-movement from (p_0) to (p_1) is divided into n parts. This can be done in various ways, of which the simplest is to suppose that the change in the price of commodity X is divided into n equal parts, that in the price of Y into n equal parts, and so on for the rest. Then the first step in the general price-movement will consist of a change, by one nth part of its total change, in the price of X, combined with one nth part of its total change in the price of Y and of the others. The second step in the general price-movement will consist of a further change in each price to an equal extent. By such means the whole of a complex change in prices can be divided into steps, just as we divided a simple change in one price into steps in our previous analysis.

Now consider the first step in the process just described, in which prices change from (p_0) to (p_{01}), as we may call it, and quantities from (q_0) to (q_{01}). The Laspeyre cost-difference, for this step, is $(p_0 - p_{01} . q_0)$. Since $p_0 - p_{01}$ is one nth part of $p_0 - p_1$, this being true for every commodity, it follows that the Laspeyre cost-difference for this step is one nth part of the total Laspeyre cost-difference which is represented by $HANK$. It can therefore be represented by a rectangle whose length is HA, and whose height is one nth part of HK, as shown. The Paasche cost-difference, for the first step, is $(p_0 - p_{01} . q_{01})$; this can be represented by a rectangle of the same height and suitable length. When we pass to the second step, from (p_{01}) to (p_{02}), its Laspeyre cost-difference is $(p_{01} - p_{02} . q_{01})$; but since all prices have changed by equal amounts in the two steps, this is equal to the Paasche cost-difference of the first step. Thus, as we carry through the representation for successive steps, we get essentially the same diagram as we got when we were considering the change in price of a single commodity (Fig. 10 in Chapter VII).

Here also, as n becomes larger, the sum of the Laspeyre cost-differences and the sum of the Paasche cost-differences draw together. The compensating variation from (p_0) to (p_1) is accordingly shown to be equal to the area $HABK$, where AB follows out a curve constructed in the manner we have been describing.

This generalized version of the *compensated demand curve* will be found in what follows to be a distinctly useful concept. But it has the odd property that it is not unique. We have built it up in a particular way, by taking successive nth parts of the total price-movement from (p_0) to (p_1). We might however have built it up in many other ways, as for instance by beginning with a series of parts of the movement in the price of X (other prices remaining stationary); and then taking parts of the movement in the price of Y (other prices remaining stationary) and so on. If we had taken a route of this sort, the steps into which the whole price-movement was divided would have been in no sense *equal*; but it would still have been true that the compensating variation from (p_0) to (p_1) lies between the sum of the Laspeyre and the sum of the Paasche cost-differences, and that the difference between these two limits becomes smaller and smaller as the number of parts into which the whole price-change is divided becomes larger and larger. Thus the compensating variation could still be represented by a strip $HABK$, with the path from A to B following out a compensated demand curve of some kind or other. The curve AB which results from one method of division of the whole price-movement would not necessarily be the same as that which results from another method of division. Our argument has nevertheless shown that the compensating variation is equal to the area $HABK$, whatever the method of division of the price-movement. Thus the areas which are cut off by the various curves must be the same. It does not matter which curve we use.[1]

3. Since the diagram which we have just been developing will be of much use to us in what follows, it will be convenient, before going farther, to make it quite general. If we had been concerned with a case in which prices 'on the whole' were rising as between (p_0) and (p_1), we could represent it, if we chose, on the same diagram as before, by making A and B (and H and K) change places. This is effectively what we do in the one-commodity theory. But in the general theory it is more convenient to adopt another way out. It is more in keeping with the general structure of the analysis if we regularly associate the points H and A with the *first* of the two positions under discussion, K and B with the *second*. If there is a general *rise* in prices from (p_0) to (p_1), both cost-differences will probably be negative; it is natural to represent these negative cost-differences by rectangles to the *left* of the axis HK. (If we do this, we can regularly show H above K, even when there is a general *rise* in prices.) The curve AB will then lie to the left of the axis, but will still (since $L \leqslant P$) be a *falling* curve, as before (Fig. 20a). The whole argument of the preceding section will then proceed as before, with the compensating variation shown as equal to the area $HABK$.

With this convention, there is no difficulty in dealing with mixed changes in prices, which may be such as to make L nega-

---

[1] Mathematicians will notice that we have done no more in the above argument than to state, in economic terms, the fundamental theorem of Riemann integration. We have already passed from transitivity to integrability. They will further notice that this question of integrability gave us no trouble, so long as we allowed no more than one price to vary. There is a significant analogy between the uniqueness of the compensated demand curve in the one-price case, and the incompatibility of higher-order inconsistency with two-term consistency in the two-goods case. But I shall not pursue this matter farther.

tive and P positive. AB will still be a falling curve, but will now cross the axis (Fig. 20b). The compensating variation will now be represented, by the same argument as before, by the *difference* between the triangles AHV and VKB.

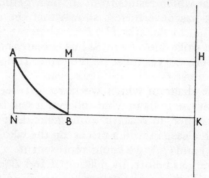

Fig. 20a.

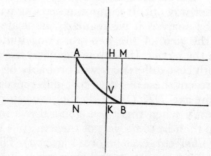

Fig. 20b.

It will be noticed that the first substitution theorem is now always represented (as was its analogue in the one-commodity theory) by the downward slope of the compensated demand curve AB.

4. The argument which we have been presenting in this chapter has been, so far, quite general; we have now to make an assumption which cuts down the applicability of our results rather drastically. All that has been said up to the present would remain true if some of the commodities whose prices were

changing were only available in large discrete units; the 'curve' AB might then have 'steps' in it, but the geometrical representation of the compensating variation would remain what we have shown it to be. From now on I shall have to assume that the commodities whose prices are changing are finely divisible, so that the compensated demand curve AB can be treated as a continuous curve.

Any continuous curve, over a sufficiently short stretch, is indistinguishable from a straight line; if therefore we assume that the changes in prices under consideration are small changes, we can treat the straight line AB as a sufficient approximation to the curve AB. It follows that we can use the simplification, which we have already employed in Chapter VIII, of representing the compensating variation by the mean of the Laspeyre and Paasche cost-differences: $C = L + \frac{1}{2}S$. Written in full, this tells us that
$$C = \tfrac{1}{2}(p_0 - p_1 \cdot q_0 + q_1).$$

As long as the price-changes under consideration are small, and as long as the commodities whose prices are changing are finely devisible, this formula is just as valid in the general theory as it is in the one-commodity theory; all the developments which we got from it can be worked out in the same way. We shall proceed, in later chapters, to follow through these developments; but for the present we must concentrate our attention upon another consequence, which has no analogue in the one-commodity theory, but which, in the general theory, is of major importance.

5. Though the above formula is only, in strictness, an approximation to the true value of the compensating variation, it becomes more and more exact as the price-change under consideration becomes smaller; consequently, for 'small' price-changes, we should demand of the formula that it satisfy the same rules as the compensating variation has been shown to satisfy. One of these rules (which was actually used in the process by which we built up the formula) was the additivity rule—that if (p_0), (p_1), and (p_2) are three sets of prices, the compensating variation in income from (p_0) to (p_2) must equal the sum of those from (p_0) to (p_1) and from (p_1) to (p_2). In any case when the formula is a close approximation to the compensating variation, the additivity rule must be satisfied by the formula.

In order to see what this implies, it will be convenient to express the changes under consideration by a rather different notation. Let us call our three positions

- (0), at which quantities (q) are purchased at prices (p),
- (1), at which quantities $(q+d_1q)$ are purchased at prices $(p-d_1p)$,
- (2), at which quantities $(q+d_2q)$ are purchased at prices $(p-d_2p)$,

all three positions being, as before, indifferent. Applying our formula to the compensating variation between (0) and (1), which we will call C_{01}, we get $C_{01} = (d_1p.q+\frac{1}{2}d_1q)$; and for the compensating variation between (0) and (2), we get

$$C_{02} = (d_2p.q+\tfrac{1}{2}d_2q).$$

For the compensating variation between (1) and (2), we get

$$C_{12} = (d_2p-d_1p.q+\tfrac{1}{2}d_1q+\tfrac{1}{2}d_2q).$$

Additivity tells us that $C_{12} = C_{02}-C_{01}$. When we write the above values for the C's into this last equation, the initial quantities (the q's) will all cancel out, leaving

$$\tfrac{1}{2}(d_2p-d_1p.d_2q+d_1q) = \tfrac{1}{2}(d_2p.d_2q)-\tfrac{1}{2}(d_1p.d_1q).$$

When we multiply out the sum-product on the left-hand side of this equation, it separates out into four terms, of which two cancel with those on the right-hand side, leaving

$$(d_2p.d_1q) = (d_1p.d_2q).$$

What this says, in words, is that the sum of the quantity-changes from (0) to (1) each being valued by the price-change of the same commodity from (0) to (2), equals the sum of the quantity-changes from (0) to (2) each being valued at the corresponding price-change from (0) to (1). I shall call this the *Reciprocity Theorem*. Though the reciprocity theorem is less generally valid than the first substitution theorem, being exactly true only in cases when commodities are finely divisible and price-changes are small, it has sufficient validity to be reckoned, in the general theory of demand, as a second main property of indifferent positions.

6. As with the first substitution theorem, the case of the reciprocity theorem which has the greatest practical importance is the simplest. Suppose that the price of one commodity only (X) varies between (o) and (1), while the price of one commodity only—but a different commodity (Y)—varies between (o) and (2). Then since $d_2 p_y$ is the only $d_2 p$ which does not vanish, the sum-product on the left of the reciprocity equation will contain no more than one term, that referring to the commodity Y; and for the same reason, that on the right will contain only one term, that referring to the commodity X. Thus the reciprocity equation reduces to the following form

$$d_2 p_y . d_1 q_y = d_1 p_x . d_2 q_x,$$

in which each side of the equation is a simple product. We may therefore divide through by the price-differences, getting

$$\frac{d_1 q_y}{d_1 p_x} = \frac{d_2 q_x}{d_2 p_y}.$$

In words, this tells us that the change in the consumption of Y that results from a unit change in the price of X (other prices constant) *equals* the change in the consumption of X which results from a unit change in the price of Y (other prices constant)—a compensating variation in income being made in each case. The cross-effects of price-changes, as we may call them, are equal.

There is of course nothing new in the reciprocity theorem in this latter form. It is established easily enough by the use of calculus, and was indeed one of the corner-stones on which the analysis of *Value and Capital* was built. I have, however, always felt that it was unsatisfactory that one was unable to give a more economic proof—especially as the mathematical proof does not make very clear the nature of the economic conditions under which we may expect the theorem to be true. Since the theorem is by no means obvious to common sense, and most economists would not be at all 'surprised' to find cases in which it was not true, close definition of the conditions on which it rests is highly desirable. I think that the present analysis does provide that definition. It is distinctly convenient to have shown that the effective conditions for the validity of the reciprocity theorem are the same as those which enable us to treat the compensated demand curve as being linear—for the latter conditions are much easier to apprehend directly. Evidently if the conditions are such that the compensated demand curve will be nearly, but not quite, linear, the reciprocity equation will be nearly, but not quite, exact.

7. The reciprocity theorem says nothing about the *sign* of the cross-effect—it may be negative or it may be positive. Retaining the definitions of *Value and Capital*, I shall say Y is a substitute for X if a fall in the price of X leads to a fall in the consumption of Y; Y is a complement of X if a fall in the price of X leads to a rise in the consumption of Y; a compensating variation in income being made, of course, in each case. Thus a fall in the price of X, combined with a compensated variation in income, which must tend to increase the consumption of X itself (by the first substitution theorem), will increase the consumption of complements, but diminish the consumption of substitutes.

The reciprocity theorem may then be put into the form of saying that the relation of substitution (and complementarity) is reciprocal. If Y is a substitute for X, X is a substitute for Y; and similarly for complements. Nevertheless it should be noticed that the theorem says something more than this mere reciprocity by classification. For substitutes to be substitutes both ways, and complements to be complements both ways, it is sufficient that the cross-effects should be the same *in sign*; they do not have to be *equal*, as the reciprocity theorem tells us that they are. The conditions for reciprocity by classification will clearly be less stringent than those for the *equality* of the cross-effects. So long as the degree of substitution (or complementarity) is considerable, we can relax the linearity condition quite considerably, and the reciprocity by classification will still hold. I think that this interpretation of the reciprocity theorem makes it much more easily acceptable; it certainly makes me feel a good deal happier about the theorem myself.

It has been said that in general the cross-effects may have either sign; but there is one special case in which this is not true. If income is being spent upon two goods only, it is impossible that those two goods should be complements. For a fall in the price of X must tend to increase the consumption of X (by the first substitution theorem); if it increases the consumption of Y, and there are no other goods in the budget, the consumer will have moved to a position in which he has more Y, and no less X; by the consistency theory, this cannot be indifferent with his initial position. Thus, in the two-goods case, the relation between the two goods must be that of substitution; a compensated price-change, if it has any effect at all, must lead to more consumption of one good and less of the other. Complementarity can only occur when there are other goods outside the group of complements, at whose expense the substitution in favour of the group of complements can take place.

XIV

SECONDARY SUBSTITUTION THEOREMS

1. The two propositions which we have now established contain within themselves nearly but not quite the whole of what can be said about the substitution effect between indifferent positions.[1] If we insist upon the maximum degree of generality, we cannot indeed go beyond the first substitution theorem. If, in our new notation, (q) purchased at prices (p), and $(q+dq)$ purchased at prices $(p-dp)$, are indifferent positions, then $(dp . dq) \geqslant 0$. This is true without the benefit of any special assumptions about divisibility or linearity, and it is unlikely that there is any more to be said which is true without any such restriction. The reciprocity theorem—if (q) purchased at (p), $(q+d_1 q)$ purchased at $(p-d_1 p)$, and $(q+d_2 q)$ purchased at $(p-d_2 p)$, are indifferent positions, then $(d_2 p . d_1 q) = (d_1 p . d_2 q)$ —can only be *proved* under strict assumptions of divisibility and linearity, which are not likely to be more than approximately satisfied in any practical application. Thus the reciprocity theorem is best regarded in practice as an indication of a relation, rather than as an exact truth. What it formally states is rather more than it leads us to believe. But this limitation on its validity does not deprive it of usefulness; so that, having once admitted a proposition of this character, it is incumbent upon us to inquire whether there are any other relations, which are worth examining, which can be established under the same, or similar, restrictions. Now it does turn out that such relations can be discovered; they are more recondite than the reciprocity theorem, and their practical importance is certainly much less, but they deserve to be inserted, at least for the sake of completeness. And it will be useful to establish them by methods of the same sort as those we have hitherto adopted, so that we should not merely stumble upon them in mathematical manipulation,

---

[1] There is another rule about the relation between indifferent positions, which we shall be discussing in Ch. XIX below, but this is concerned with the whole quantities consumed, not merely with the substitution effect.

but should be able to assess the validity—as it turns out, the rather limited validity—which it is proper to attribute to them.

These secondary substitution theorems are best approached by a further investigation of the exact implication of the linearity assumption. For this purpose, let us return for a moment to the elementary case in which the price of one commodity only is varying. If the demand curve for this commodity is linear, the ratio of change in quantity to change in price, which is the slope of the demand curve, is constant. Thus if consumption expands from q to $q+dq$ when price falls from p to $p-dp$, consumption will expand from q to $q+k\,dq$ when price falls from p to $p-k\,dp$, k being a fraction. In words, consumption responds to price-changes at a constant rate. Now if we generalize this conception for a multiple price-change, it is natural to say that the demand function for each of the commodities affected is linear, if a change in prices from (p) to $(p-k\,dp)$, where k is the same for all commodities, will change the consumption of *each* commodity considered by the same fraction k of the full change which would have taken place if prices had changed to $(p-dp)$. Thus the demand functions are linear, if the price-set $(p-k\,dp)$ calls forth the quantity-set $(q+k\,dq)$, whatever the value of k. Each quantity consumed will then be responding to the multiple price-change at a constant rate.

This is the natural mathematical generalization of linearity, though it should be noticed that it is rather more than we had to assume for the purposes of the reciprocity theorem. The linearity which was necessary for those purposes was sufficiently ensured if an appropriately weighted average of the quantities (q) changed at a constant rate in response to regular price-changes; here we are going to assume that the quantity of *each* commodity changes regularly. I would freely admit that we can hardly expect to find such complete regularity in practice, even over the range of a small change in prices; but it is plausible to argue that the actual set of quantities consumed by a representative consumer at an intermediate price-set will often differ only a little from the 'regular' quantities. If so, it would probably be the case that the 'regular' position, corresponding to an intermediate price-set, would itself satisfy the indifference tests with respect to either end-position, or to any position indifferent with them; for it will be remembered that if A and B are indifferent, the indifference tests will usually be satisfied, not merely as between A and B, but also as between A and any position in the near neighbourhood of B. It therefore seems worth while to inquire what consequences follow if the 'regular' positions, which are constructed by means of the linearity assumption, are near enough to the actual positions to satisfy the same tests as the corresponding actual positions should satisfy. Since it is only the quantities of the commodities whose prices are changing which are to move 'regularly', we must apply the indifference tests in the form which eliminates quantities of other commodities—that is to say, in the classical form of the first substitution theorem.

2. If as a first step, we apply the first substitution theorem to a position A and to a position intermediate between A and B, when A is indifferent to B, we find that we get no new result. For if (q) purchased at (p), and $(q+dq)$ purchased at $(p-dp)$, are indifferent positions, and we take an intermediate position $(q+k\,dq)$ purchased at $(p-k\,dp)$, the substitution effect between the first of the end-positions and the intermediate position comes out as

$$k^2(dp\,.\,dq),$$

while that between the second of the end-positions and the intermediate position comes out as

$$(1-k)^2(dp\,.\,dq),$$

and both of these are necessarily $\geqslant 0$ as soon as it is given that the end-positions are indifferent.

Suppose, however, that we go on to apply the same reasoning to a triad, such as we used in the development of the reciprocity theorem. Let us consider the substitution effect between (0), which, as before, is (q) purchased at (p), and (T) which is a position 'regularly' intermediate between (1) and (2). Suppose that (T) divides (1) and (2) in the ratio $\lambda:\mu$ (where $\lambda+\mu = 1$). Then (T) is $(q+\lambda\,d_1q+\mu\,d_2q)$ purchased at $(p-\lambda\,d_1p-\mu\,d_2p)$, λ and μ being the same for all commodities. The first substitution theorem, applied to (0) and (T), gives

$$(\lambda\,d_1p+\mu\,d_2p\,.\,\lambda\,d_1q+\mu\,d_2q) \geqslant 0,$$

an inequality which can be used to develop some new properties.

Multiplying it out, it becomes

$$\lambda_2(d_1 p . d_1 q) + \lambda\mu(d_2 p . d_1 q) + \lambda\mu(d_1 p . d_2 q) + \mu^2(d_2 p . d_2 q),$$

and each of these terms is readily recognizable. The coefficient of λ^2 is the direct substitution effect between (0) and (1); call it S_{01}. The coefficient of μ^2 is the direct substitution effect between (0) and (2); call it S_{02}. The coefficients of $\lambda\mu$ are the cross-effects, which the reciprocity theorem maintains to be equal; let us call them R. Thus the first substitution theorem, applied to (0) and (T), tells us that

$$\lambda^2 S_{01} + 2\lambda\mu R + \mu^2 S_{02} \geqslant 0,$$

a relation which tells us just a little more than we knew before.

Certainly it is not much. We know that S_{01} and S_{02} are $\geqslant 0$, so that the first and third terms in the above expression cannot be negative. If we confine our attention to positions (T) that lie *between* (1) and (2), λ and μ must be positive, and the above condition is necessarily satisfied if R is positive. It is only when R is negative that we get additional information, in the form of a limit on the size of the negative values that R may take. The existence of this limit on the size of the cross-effect is the effective lesson which we learn from the Second Substitution Theorem.

It is, however, formally true that large positive values of the cross-effect are ruled out by the same condition, if we admit negative values of the ratio $\lambda:\mu$. But if this ratio is negative, (T) lies *outside* the range (1) to (2), and to assume even approximate linearity outside the range between two neighbouring positions is far more dubious than to assume linearity within it. I do not think that we can put any reliance upon the formal exclusion of positive values for R.

If the (0T) substitution effect is to be positive for any position (T), dividing (1) and (2) in any ratio, the limit upon the size of R can be easily calculated. For since $S_{01} \geqslant 0$,

$$S_{01}(\lambda^2 S_{01} + 2\lambda\mu R + \mu^2 S_{02}) = (\lambda S_{01} + \mu R)^2 + \mu^2(S_{01} . S_{02} - R^2) \geqslant 0.$$

The first term in this last expression cannot be negative, but will be zero for a suitable value of $\lambda:\mu$. Thus the (0T) substitution effect will be $\geqslant 0$, for all values of $\lambda:\mu$, if $R^2 < S_{01} . S_{02}$, but not otherwise. The cross-effect must not be greater, *in size*, than the geometric mean of the direct substitution effects. This is the second substitution theorem.

3. As in the case of the reciprocity theorem, the simplest case to which the present analysis can be applied is that in which the price of one good only, X, changes from (o) to (1), and that of another good only, Y, changes from (o) to (2). R will then represent the cross-effect of the price of X on the demand for Y (or of the price of Y on the demand for X). S_{01} will represent the direct effect of the price of X on the demand for X; S_{02} the direct effect of the price of Y on the demand for Y. R is positive when X and Y are complements; negative when they are substitutes. Thus the second substitution theorem sets a limit on the degree of substitutability between X and Y which is consistent with given direct effects of the prices of X and Y on the demands for the same commodities. That there should be such a limit is conformable to common sense, for it is evident that X and Y cannot be highly substitutable for one another unless each has a demand which is highly elastic with respect to its own price (that of the other remaining constant). What we have been doing in this chapter is to put this simple point into more precise, and more general, terms.

The 'theoretical' limit upon the possible degree of complementarity is much less agreeable to common sense; it is a particular merit of the approach to the theorem which is here adopted that it shows why we do not have to take this limit seriously. It is indeed a good example of the way in which a blind adherence to standard mathematical methods sometimes produces nonsense results.

4. The second substitution theorem is not the only proposition of its type which exists; though it is the most important of such propositions. We can, in an exactly similar manner, start from *four* given indifferent positions, (o), (1), (2), and (3); and then proceed to construct a position (T) 'regularly' intermediate between (1), (2), and (3). (T) would thus come out as the quantities $(q + \lambda\, d_1 q + \mu\, d_2 q + \nu\, d_3 q)$, purchased at prices

$$(p - \lambda\, d_1 p - \mu\, d_2 p - \nu\, d_3 p),$$

where $\lambda + \mu + \nu = 1$. The (oT) substitution effect then gives

$$\lambda^2 S_{01} + \mu^2 S_{02} + \nu^2 S_{03} + 2\mu\nu R_{23} + 2\nu\lambda R_{31} + 2\lambda\mu R_{12} \geqslant o.$$

If this is to be true for all λ, μ, ν, it is not merely necessary that the second substitution theorem should hold for each triad (012), (023), (031); a further inequality, of determinantal form, is also necessary. Though the meaning of this inequality is not very apparent, it does have its uses, as we shall find when we come back to the matter at a later stage.[1] And the same holds for the further conditions of still higher orders which can be ground out by further applications of the same technique.

[1] See below, p. 159.

XV

THE INCOME EFFECT

1. We are now in a position to pass on to the next stage of our inquiry, which can be seen to have a wider scope than it appeared to have when we first saw it in the distance. At the corresponding stage of the elementary theory, it will be remembered, we had established a law—the downward slope of the compensated demand curve—which held between indifferent positions; we next proceeded to show that a corresponding law—the downward slope of the uncompensated demand curve—continued to hold (not without exceptions, but without exceptions of practical importance) between the non-indifferent positions in which we were more interested. Here, in the generalized theory, we have *three* rules which have been established between indifferent positions—those expressed in the first and second substitution theorems and the reciprocity theorem. Our task in this chapter must be to examine how far these three theorems require to be modified when we allow for the Income Effect.

The first substitution theorem maintains that when prices change from (p) to $(p-dp)$, and there is a compensating variation in income, quantities consumed will change from (q) to $(q+dq)$, when the increments are such as to make $S = (dp \cdot dq) \geqslant 0$. If there is no compensating variation in income, there will be an additional set of increments of consumption, due to the off-setting of the compensating variation; suppose that consumption then changes to $(q+dq+\delta q)$, so that (δq) is the set of income effects. Then the generalization of the law of demand, to which we seem to be led, would assert that

$$(dp \cdot dq + \delta q) = (dp \cdot dq) + (dp \cdot \delta q) = S + I$$

will be *generally* positive. This will clearly be true (as in the elementary theory) if I is positive; or if I is negative, but not large enough to outweigh the positive substitution effect S. We are thus led to make a general examination of the properties of the Total Income Effect I. How far can we rely upon its behaving in such a way as to leave us with $S+I \geqslant 0$, at least as a general rule?

2. It will be remembered that when we were considering the analogous problem in the elementary theory, we found it useful to have at our disposal an alternative approach, which we called the cost-difference method.[1] If, instead of an adjustment in income by the amount of the compensating variation, we introduced an adjustment by the amount of the initial (or Laspeyre) cost-difference, it could be shown (in the elementary theory) that the resulting change in consumption must still proceed in the orthodox direction. A corresponding theorem is valid in the present, more general, setting. Suppose that prices change from (p) to $(p-dp)$, while the consumer's income is adjusted by the amount of the cost-difference $(dp \cdot q)$; consumption then changes from (q) to $(q+d'q)$. The consumer's income, in the new situation, is $(p-dp \cdot q)$; this must equal his expenditure $(p-dp \cdot q+d'q)$; so that $(p-dp \cdot d'q) = 0$, or $(p \cdot d'q) = (dp \cdot d'q)$. But if the set $(d'q)$ have a zero value at the new prices $(p-dp)$, they cannot have a negative value at the old prices (p).[2] Thus $(p \cdot d'q) \geqslant 0$, so that $(dp \cdot d'q) \geqslant 0$. Thus there is an analogue of the first substitution theorem, which holds if income is adjusted by the cost-difference, instead of being adjusted by the compensating variation.

We may accordingly say that the total effect of a change in prices, unaccompanied by change in income, may be divided into two parts (S and I) by the selection of an intermediate position in which income changes by the amount of the compensating variation; *or* it can be divided into two parts (S' and I') by the selection of an intermediate position in which income changes by the amount of the cost-difference. Each of the two substitution effects (S and S') is necessarily $\geqslant 0$; each of the two income-effects is the pure effect of a change in income at constant prices. The only difference between I and I' concerns the amount by which income is supposed to have changed. Evidently it will be sufficient, for the establishment of the generalized law of demand, if we can show that either I or I' is

---

[1] Cf. above, Ch. VII.
[2] For it is impossible that $(p_0 \cdot q_0) > (p_0 \cdot q_1)$ while $(p_1 \cdot q_0) = (p_1 \cdot q_1)$, by the consistency test.

generally positive—or that, if negative, it is likely to be small. We have a choice between routes.

3. Whichever route we adopt, the income-effect which has now to be studied is the pure effect of a change in income; but our concern is with what we have called the total income effect, which is a combination of the separate income-effects on the separate commodities. As before, we shall describe a commodity which is such that its consumption falls when income rises as an 'inferior good'; goods which are not inferior being described as 'normal'. If we keep to the assumption that we have maintained throughout—that all income is 'spent', or that saving is reckoned as a purchased commodity—a rise in income must result in a rise in total expenditure. Thus though some of the articles in the consumer's budget may be inferior, inferiority of some goods must be more than balanced by normality elsewhere.

It will however be noticed that it is only those goods the prices of which are changing that enter into the total income effect; so that it is perfectly possible that all these goods are inferior—we have to allow for the case in which the complex price-change that we are considering relates entirely to a bunch of inferior goods. The ordinary application, even of the generalized theory we are now considering, is to a set of changes in the prices of a group of goods, not to changes which affect all the prices that confront the consumer.

As a first step in the analysis of the total income effect I (or I'), it will be convenient to consider the case in which each dp is positive, so that all prices that are changing are falling—though not at all necessarily to the same extent. In this case the compensating variation (or the cost-difference) is necessarily positive, so that the income-effect comes about by an *increase* in income. If all the goods whose prices are changing are normal, each separate income-effect δq will be positive; since each dp is positive, the total income effect is the sum of a set of positive terms and must itself be positive. If all the goods whose prices change are inferior, I must be negative. If some are normal and some inferior, the sign of I depends upon the relative strengths of the separate income-effects (weighted by the separate price-changes).

Similarly, in the case when all the prices that change are rising, the compensating variation will be negative (as also the cost-difference); the income effect is brought about by a *fall* in income. If all the goods whose prices change are normal, each separate income-effect will be negative, but since each of the corresponding price-differences is negative, their product is positive; I is again the sum of a set of positive terms, and must be positive, as before. I will be negative, as before, if all the goods whose prices change are inferior; and will in general, as before, represent the balance of normality over inferiority.

Accordingly, so long as all prices that change are changing in the same direction, we get the same significance for the sign of I. So long as there is a balance of normality over inferiority, I must be positive; and since there is the general tendency for normality to be dominant, over the whole range of goods consumed, we should expect to find that the required balance was realized, in most of the price-changes that we are called upon to consider. In all such cases, the *generalized law of demand*,

$$S+I = (dp \cdot dq + \delta q) \geqslant 0,$$

must hold. Prices and quantities must move, in this sense, in opposite directions.

The generalized law, like the elementary law, is subject to exception; but the only exception which is so far thrown up by our analysis concerns the case in which the price-changing goods are all of them, or most of them, inferior. It is possible that the whole group of goods which are inferior for our consumer may account for a fairly large proportion of his expenditure; if the prices of all these goods change in the same direction (without there being any other price-change) the negative I which is set up may be rather large. If the total substitution effect between these goods and the rest is fairly small, it is then possible that $I+S$ may be negative. This is the natural generalization of the Giffen case; in one sense it has to be taken a little more seriously than the Giffen case itself. For the share in consumer's expenditure going upon all inferior goods taken together may be much larger than that going upon any particular inferior good, so that a large negative I is more possible in the generalized theory than it was in the elementary theory. But the kind of price-change which would call forth a negative effect of this character would be very peculiar indeed; it is the kind of thing which has to be invented just to cause trouble! So far as we are concerned with price-changes which are one-directional, the generalized law of demand seems then to be subject to little more exception than the elementary Marshallian law.

4. The mixed case—in which some prices change in one direction, some in the other—is a little more original. Here also there is a presumption that the generalized law of demand will usually hold; but the law is subject to an exception of a different character.

As before, we should begin by distinguishing those cases in which the income-effect is due to a rise in real income from those in which it is due to a fall. This is a less simple matter than previously, because the compensating variation and the cost-difference are no longer bound to be of the same sign. It is always true that $C \geqslant L$, but this leaves it possible that C may be positive and L negative, though it is not possible that L may be positive and C negative. But since C and L differ by (approximately) $\frac{1}{2}S$, if C is positive and L negative the magnitude of either must be small relatively to the substitution effect S; the income-effect which either calls forth must therefore be small relatively to the substitution effect. There can be no exception to the law of demand in such a case; we may accordingly concentrate our attention on cases in which C and L do go in the same direction.

If C and L are positive, the income effect (as before) is brought about by an increase in income. If all the price-changing goods are normal, each separate income-effect will be positive; each δq is positive, but it no longer follows that I is positive, because the dp's vary in sign. Thus inferiority ceases to be the only possible cause of negative I. We have a new exception to deal with, which did not arise in the other cases.

The nature of this exception is most conveniently defined in terms of 'income-elasticities'. η_x, the income-elasticity of demand for commodity X, is the ratio of the proportionate increase in consumption of X to the proportionate increase in income which calls it forth. If prices are changing from (p) to $(p-dp)$, total income is $(p \cdot q)$, while the cost-difference is $(dp \cdot q)$, so that the proportionate change in income, which calls forth the income-effect, is $(dp \cdot q)/(p \cdot q)$. The proportionate change in the consumption of commodity X is thus $\eta_x(dp.q)/(p.q)$; and the separate income-effect on commodity X is $\eta_x q_x(dp.q)/(p.q)$. Multiplying by the price-change dp_x, and summing over all commodities, we get (since we are using the cost-difference method)

$$I = \frac{(dp.q)(dp.\eta q)}{(p.q)}$$

as a general formula for the total income effect.

This formula is valid in all cases; when all prices are changing in the same direction, we can write $(dp.\eta q) = \bar{\eta}(dp.q)$, so that $\bar{\eta}$ is a weighted average of the income-elasticities of the price-changing commodities. Then $(p.q)I = \bar{\eta}L^2$, and I can only be negative if $\bar{\eta}$ is negative, which is what we have found.

In the mixed case, it is best to collect the price-falling and price-rising commodities into separate groups. In the price-falling group, let the sum of their (positive) cost-differences be L_1, and their average income-elasticity η_1; in the price-rising group, let the sum of their (negative) cost-differences be $-L_2$, and their average income-elasticity η_2. Then

$$(p.q)I = (L_1-L_2)(\eta_1 L_1-\eta_2 L_2)$$
$$= \tfrac{1}{2}(\eta_1+\eta_2)(L_1-L_2)^2+\tfrac{1}{2}(\eta_1-\eta_2)(L_1^2-L_2^2).$$

Thus the total income-effect now falls into two parts, of which the first is necessarily positive if the average of all the income-elasticities is positive, while the other depends upon the difference between the average income-elasticities of the two groups. If $\eta_1 = \eta_2$, the second term disappears, and we get no possibility of a negative I unless there is a dominance of inferiority among the price-changing goods as a whole. But if there is a great difference between η_1 and η_2, which goes in the opposite direction to the net cost-difference, then the second term in the above formula may be negative; it may conceivably be so negative as to make I negative as a whole, even if there is no inferiority anywhere.

5. Thus in the mixed case, the total income effect may be regarded as having two parts, of which the first (I_1) will only go negative if there is a general dominance of inferiority among the price-changing goods (as before). The second (I_2) will go negative if there is a special sort of asymmetry between the

price-falling and price-rising goods, with respect to their income-elasticities. Either I_1 or I_2 may be responsible, in extreme cases, for an exception to the generalized law of demand, since either may be so negative as to make $S+I$ negative. But negative I_1, leading to negative $S+I$, is nothing more than a generalization of the Giffen case, and needs no further investigation. Negative I_2 is a different story.

A case in which the law of demand would break down, for this new reason, is the following. Suppose that there is a sharp fall in the prices of a large group of necessaries (with income-elasticity zero), and a rise in the prices of a group of luxuries (with high income-elasticity). Suppose that the gain from the fall more than compensates for the loss from the rise, so that there is a gain in real income. The gain in real income will not induce any increase in consumption of the necessaries, though it will of the luxuries, in spite of their prices having risen. The income-effect will accordingly be negative, in spite of the fact that none of the goods are inferior. In order that there should be an exception to the law of demand, from this cause, this negative income effect must outweight the substitution effect. Now it is intelligible that there should be no substitution in favour of the necessaries, as a result of their fall in price; inelasticity against income may well involve inelasticity against price also. If the two groups of goods comprise all the goods in the consumer's budget, and if the prices of the various goods within each group move proportionately to one another, this lack of substitution effect on the side of the necessaries will imply a lack of substitution effect on the side of the luxuries also. Thus if all these conditions are satisfied, the law of demand will fail. But notice how the conditions which are necessary in order to make this seem at all probable have piled up. If the two groups do not include all the goods which are available for consumption, there is likely to be a substitution effect against the luxuries, which have risen in price, in favour of the third group, which has not. If the rises in price of the luxuries are non-proportional, there is likely to be a substitution effect in favour of those luxuries which have risen less against those which have risen more. These possibilities have to be excluded, on top of the very special kind of price-change with which we started, in order to make a plausible case for an exception to the law of demand along the new route.

I think we may conclude that the new exception, though perhaps more interesting than the Giffen exception, is hardly more formidable. In the sense in which the elementary law of demand is valid, the generalized law seems to be valid also.

6. Before going farther, it will be useful to emphasize just what it is that we have so far established. We have shown that if prices change from (p_0) to (p_1), and quantities consumed from (q_0) to (q_1), the sum-product $(p_0-p_1.q_1-q_0)$ will be positive or zero, (i) necessarily if income has been adjusted by the amount of the compensating variation or cost-difference, (ii) with high probability if income is constant. Let us however suppose that we are comparing two positions between which income neither remains constant nor changes in either of the particular ways mentioned. Is there any extension of the law of demand which will remain valid in this still more general case?

It is clear at once that the rule, as stated, will not remain valid against *any* change in income. This can readily be checked by reference to the elementary law, which is itself a special case of the more general law to which we have now come. Other prices being constant, a fall in the price of X will lead to an increase in the demand for X, when income is constant, with no more than the Giffen exception; if income is reduced by the amount of the compensating variation (or cost-difference) not even that exception can occur. If X is normal, a rise in income will further increase the demand for X, so that the law of demand will remain formally valid, even though income has not moved in any of the stated ways. But a reduction in income will reduce the demand for X, and a sufficient reduction in income must offset the substitution effect and cause the demand for X to diminish in spite of the fall in price. Thus the elementary law of demand (and the same must clearly be true for the generalized law) cannot remain true however income varies; the changes in income which are consistent with its truth must be of the 'right' character.

This is, for some purposes, a difficulty; but there is a way round it. A change in income, accompanied by a change in all prices in the same proportion as income has changed, will leave the opportunities that confront the consumer the same as before; it is reasonable to assume that the quantities he consumes will be unaffected by a change of this special character. Thus if income changes from Y_0 to Y_1 while prices change from (p_0) to (p_1), the changes in the (q)'s will be the same as if prices had changed from (p_0) to $\dfrac{Y_0}{Y_1}(p_1)$ without any change in income. Thus if we 'deflate' prices by an index of income, the law of demand will hold in terms of the deflated prices, even though it might not hold in terms of prices that had not been deflated in this way. By this device we are enabled to dispense with any special assumption about the change (or absence of change) of income.

7. So far, however, we have been working in terms of the behaviour of the individual consumer; but as always, the theory of individual demand is only interesting as a step towards the construction of a theory of market demand. In this connexion the last point which we have been making is of particular importance. For we have no difficulty in showing that the law of demand will apply to a group of consumers, just as well as to an individual consumer, so long as all their incomes remain constant while prices change. The market S is the sum of individual S's; since they tend to be positive, it must do so also. The market I is the sum of individual I's; thus it can only go negative for the same reasons as may make individual I's go negative. Indeed, for the market I to be negative, there must be a balance of negativeness among the individual I's that compose it. As in the elementary theory, this is less likely than that some individual I's will be negative. The probability of exceptional cases is diminished when we take a large group of heterogeneous consumers together.

If there is a change in incomes, alongside the change in prices, we have to be more careful. If all the incomes changed in the same proportion, we could use the device of 'deflating', and the law of demand would still hold in terms of the deflated prices. But if, as will usually happen, the incomes of the various consumers do not change in the same proportion, we have to introduce a new qualification.

It will still be useful to deflate by the average change in income, so that the problem is reduced to one in which the total of income is kept constant, though it is redistributed among the individuals composing the group.[1] Such redistribution can be regarded as setting up a third kind of income-effect, which increases the demands for those commodities for which the gainers have a high income-elasticity, and diminishes the demands for those for which the losers have a high income-elasticity. If these two sets of commodities are much the same, these two movements will cancel out, and the redistribution income-effect will be inconsiderable. But if the gainers buy more of quite different commodities than those on which the losers economize, the total quantities consumed will be different from what they would have been if all incomes had changed in the same proportion—the quantities of some being up and others down. If the prices of the commodities for which demand is expanded were mainly falling, or the prices of the other set were mainly rising, the redistribution effect will tend to increase I, so that it will confirm the validity of the law of demand. But in the opposite case, the redistribution effect on I will be negative, so that it introduces a new possibility of an exception to the law. But here again, the disturbance due to redistribution must be rather great, and must be of rather a special character, if the possible exception is to become actual.

This last exception, which we have mentioned for completeness, is of course a possible exception to the Marshallian law itself. If the price of X falls (other prices constant), while the total income of consumers remains constant, it is always possible that the consumption of X may fall, if income is redistributed from X-likers to X-dislikers. We have done no more than generalize this obvious consideration.

The reader may nevertheless be asking what is left of a general rule, which is subject to exceptions of so many varieties. I think that there is a good deal left. We have been striving, it will be realized, for the maximum degree of generality that is consistent

[1] If the number of individuals in the group has changed, the preference hypothesis can only be interpreted to mean that the original group contained a individuals with one type of preference-scale, b with a second, c with a third, and so on; and that the number of individuals in each group has increased in the same proportion. On this interpretation, we should deflate *prices* by *average* income, so as to keep the income of the representative consumer the same; and we should deflate *quantities* by the number of individuals.

with the maintenance of the preference hypothesis. Even when we do so, we find no more than three possible sorts of exception —those due to inferior goods, to commodity asymmetry, and to asymmetrical effects of redistribution. In many (perhaps most) applications that we shall want to make, some (perhaps all) of these possibilities will be ruled out by the conditions of the problem. In the great majority of cases, which are such that it is proper to assume unchanging wants, one would expect the law to hold.

8. Something remains to be said about the other propositions which were enunciated in the preceding chapters—the reciprocity theorem and the second substitution theorem. Here too we may ask what becomes of the rules in question when we allow for the income effect—though we shall not find it necessary to investigate these problems in the same detail. The reciprocity theorem, it will be remembered, depended strictly upon the transitivity property of indifference; thus it can only be reached by the compensating variation method, having no analogue in terms of cost-difference. So far as the second substitution theorem depends on the reciprocity theorem, the same is true in its case also.

Let us recall our previous statement of the reciprocity theorem. If prices change from (p) to $(p-d_1 p)$ and again to $(p-d_2 p)$, with a compensating variation in income in each case, the quantities consumed will change from (q) to $(q+d_1 q)$ and $(q+d_2 q)$, which are such that

$$(d_2 p . d_1 q) = (d_1 p . d_2 q).$$

If there is no compensating variation in either case, but income remains constant, there is an income-effect to be allowed for, which may be written $(\delta_1 q)$ and $(\delta_2 q)$ in the two cases. Thus consumption changes to $(q+d_1 q+\delta_1 q)$ and $(q+d_2 q+\delta_2 q)$. If the reciprocity theorem were to hold, even approximately, when income is constant, the cross-effects

$$(d_2 p . d_1 q+\delta_1 q) \quad \text{and} \quad (d_1 p . d_2' q+\delta_2 q)$$

must be approximately equal. Now these cross-effects divide into cross-substitution effects, as written above, which are equal, and cross-income effects, which need further consideration.

As before, it will be convenient to express them in terms of income-elasticities. Application of the same method as we used previously shows that

$$(d_2 p . \delta_1 q) = (d_1 p . q)(d_2 p . \eta q)/(p . q) = \eta_2(d_1 p . q)(d_2 p . q)/(p . q),$$
$$(d_1 p . \delta_2 q) = (d_2 p . q)(d_1 p . \eta q)/(p . q) = \eta_1(d_2 p . q)(d_1 p . q)/(p . q),$$

where η_1 is the average of the income-elasticities of the commodities, weighted by the cost-differences due to the first price-change $(d_1 p)$ and η_2 is the average of the income-elasticities, weighted by the cost-differences due to the second price-change $(d_2 p)$. There is in general no reason why η_1 and η_2 should be equal, so that there is in general no reason why the two cross-income effects should be the same.

We may accordingly conclude that for the reciprocity theorem to hold, approximately, when income is constant, it is in general necessary for the cross-income effect to be small relatively to the cross-substitution effect. In the most important application of the reciprocity theorem, to the substitution-complementarity relation between a pair of commodities, this will probably happen if the commodities are strong substitutes, or strong complements. But if they are only weak substitutes, or weak complements, the equality between the cross-substitution effects may well be masked by inequality between the cross-income effects on income-elasticities. This was set out in full in *Value and Capital* (pp. 48–49).

9. In the case of the second substitution theorem, we can allow for income effects at the expense of much less qualification. It is just as legitimate to assume linearity of the uncompensated demand functions as of the compensated (for small-price-changes); thus if income remains constant, we can still say that a change in prices from (p) to $(p - \lambda\, d_1 p - \mu\, d_2 p)$ will change quantities from (q) to $(q + \lambda\, d_1 q + \mu\, d_2 q)$, the (dq)'s here including both income and substitution effects. If we assume the truth of the generalized law of demand, which allows for income as well as substitution effects, we shall have

$$(\lambda\, d_1 p + \mu\, d_2 p . \lambda\, d_1 q + \mu\, d_2 q) \geqslant 0.$$

If this is to be true for all values of the ratio $\lambda : \mu$, we must have

$$4(d_1 p . d_1 q)(d_2 p . d_2 q) \geqslant [(d_1 p . d_2 q) + (d_2 p . d_1 q)]^2.$$

The arithmetic mean of the (combined) cross-effects cannot

exceed the geometric mean of the corresponding direct effects. In terms of the relation between a pair of substitutes, this gives us a connexion between the four 'demand curves' (1) quantity of X against price of X, (2) quantity of Y against price of Y, (3) quantity of Y against price of X, (4) quantity of X against price of Y. The arithmetic mean between the slopes of (3) and (4) cannot be greater in magnitude than the geometric mean between the slopes of (1) and (2). Granted the truth of the generalized law of demand, this extension of the second substitution theorem will be very generally valid.

XVI

SUBSTITUTES AND COMPLEMENTS IN VALUATION THEORY

1. We next come to that part of the generalized theory of demand which corresponds to the inversion of the demand curve into the marginal valuation curve. Here then, instead of treating quantities consumed as dependent on prices, we inquire into the dependence of the marginal valuations of commodities consumed on the quantities of those commodities. In a competitive market, each consumer makes the marginal valuation of each commodity to him equal to its price; thus in the market sense, the valuation approach enables us to treat the prices paid by consumers as dependent upon the supplies available. The dependence of prices on quantities can of course be worked out, though at the expense of rather heavy mathematics, by solving the system of equations given by equality between demand and supply in the various markets;[1] the valuation approach enables us to short-circuit all this mathematics, reducing the whole matter to readily intelligible economic sense.

That such an approach is possible, in general, is suggested by the form in which we have written the indifference theorems. The first substitution theorem told us that the change in demand which results from a compensated change in prices must be such as to make $(dp \cdot dq) \geqslant 0$; the reciprocity theorem (within the limits of its applicability) told us that the changes in demand which follow upon two different compensated changes in prices must be such that $(d_1 p \cdot d_2 q) = (d_2 p \cdot d_1 q)$; the second substitution theorem (with similar restrictions) that

$$(d_1 p \cdot d_2 q)^2 \leqslant (d_1 p \cdot d_1 q)(d_2 p \cdot d_2 q).$$

Now in all these formulae the parts played by prices and quantities (p's and q's) are exactly symmetrical. We could change p's into q's and q's into p's and the formulae would be unchanged.

[1] As was done, for some simple cases, in *Value and Capital*, ch. v; and more fully, in the Mathematical Appendix to that book, pp. 315–19. See also J. L. Mosak, *General Equilibrium Theory in International Trade*, ch. 2.

So far we have been reading the formulae as giving rules for the dependence of quantities on prices; but if we could read them as expressing dependence of prices on quantities, the rules we should get would be exactly parallel. Thus the whole theory looks capable of being stood on its head. What we have now to see is with what precautions the somersault can be performed.

2. Let us begin, as in our former discussion of the law of demand, by comparing the positions of a particular consumer at A and at B, which are such that at A he purchases quantities (q_0) at prices (p_0), while at B he purchases quantities (q_1) at prices (p_1). But whereas we previously assumed that he moved from A to B as a consequence of the change in prices, let us now assume that the movement has come about as the result of some change in unspecified economic variables (such as technical improvements or a change in the supply of the factors of production). Assuming, as before, that preferences remain unchanged, and that the consumer is operating on a competitive market, let us inquire what change in prices, from (p_0) to (p_1), is consistent with the change in quantities from (q_0) to (q_1), now taken to be given. This is the general way of posing the problem to which we seem to be led by the valuation approach.

In imitation of our previous procedure, we should begin by looking for an intermediate position β, indifferent to A, but in some way comparable with B. And here at once we run into a difficulty. We should like to be able to define the position β as one that is indifferent to A, but contains the same quantities as B; but that is impossible, for if β contains the same quantities as B, it will be B, and will not be an intermediate position. The search for the intermediate position, on which the whole analysis depends, seems to break down at once.

The difficulty can however be overcome in the following way. We must confine our attention to cases in which there exists at least one commodity which has a price that does not change between A and B. Since for this commodity $p_0 = p_1$, its quantity will not appear in the sum-product of the substitution theorem; variations in its quantity will not affect that sum-product. This particular commodity (it can be a group, even a large group, of commodities, so long as all their prices are constant) proves to play very much the same part in our valuation theory as the *Money* which figures in Marshall's theory of the consumer. It is of course the same as the 'background commodity' which figured in our exposition of the elementary theory, elementary because it admitted only one commodity into the foreground. Here we can have several commodities in the foreground, but we cannot get on without some commodity remaining in the background, with the spot light off it.

Though it is a little awkward to talk about the consumer 'spending' a part of his 'income' on 'money' (even though we mean no more than that it is not spent on the foreground commodities), there is much to be said for keeping Marshall's name, as an indication that we are following in his footsteps. And the fact that what we are determining, in accordance with this convention, are prices in terms of 'money', makes the name in another way very appropriate.

Let us then say that the fixed price of the 'money' commodity is unity. Let us represent the quantity of 'money' in any particular budget by m, marking it out in this way from the quantities of other commodities, which are still represented by q's. The quantities of commodities consumed at A are therefore to be represented by $q_{0x}, q_{0y}, q_{0z},..., m_0$; or (q_0, m_0) for short. The quantities of commodities consumed at B will be similarly (q_1, m_1). Now if (q_1, m_1) is preferred to (q_0, m_0), we should be able to adjust it so as to make it indifferent to (q_0, m_0) by changing the quantity of money which it contains. By this means we could define a collection $\beta(q_1, m')$, which is indifferent to A, though it contains the same quantities of all commodities except money as the collection B. We have then divided the whole movement from A to B into (i) a movement from A to β, which is a movement between two indifferent positions, (ii) a movement from β to B, which involves no change except an increase in the quantity of money. The first of these movements is a substitution effect, while the second has already been shown (in Chapter VIII) to have a close analogy with the income effect of 'price into quantity' theory.

On the whole, the analogy between the two approaches is very close; but before proceeding farther, we should notice one way in which it does not hold. When we were considering a *given* change in prices, from $A(p_0)$ to $B(p_1)$, it was possible to *prove* the

existence of an intermediate position b, indifferent to A and
such that it could be bought at (p_1) prices.[1] No such proof can
be given in the present case. It is clearly possible that the
amounts of the q-goods in B may be so large that a reduction
of m_1 to zero would still leave the B-collection preferred to the
A-collection. Thus if the device we are here employing is to be
effective, the changes in quantities of the q-goods must not be
too large; or, what comes to the same thing, the amount of
'money' in the consumer's budget must not be too small. Thus
in the valuation theory we have no general assurance that the
intermediate position exists; but the theory is only valid if it
exists, and this sets a limit on the range of problems to which
valuation theory can be properly applied.

3. We may now proceed to see what new light can be got
from the indifference theorems, when they are considered in
terms of the valuation approach. For this purpose we can confine our attention to the relation between two positions which
are known to be indifferent; for the present we shall not involve
ourselves in any ambiguity if we allow ourselves to call these two
positions $A(q_0, m_0)$ and $B(q_1, m_1)$.

The fundamental relations between these two positions are
given, as before, by the indifference tests—from which, as
before, the indifference theorems are derived. In our present
notation (with money separated out) the indifference tests will
be written

$$(p_0 \cdot q_0) + m_0 \leqslant (p_0 \cdot q_1) + m_1, \quad (p_1 \cdot q_1) + m_1 \leqslant (p_1 \cdot q_0) + m_0,$$

whence it follows that

$$(p_0 \cdot q_1 - q_0) \geqslant m_0 - m_1 \geqslant (p_1 \cdot q_1 - q_0).$$

Now since A and B are indifferent, $m_0 - m_1$ is the maximum
amount of money which the consumer can give up while passing
from (q_0) to (q_1) without being made worse off. This is the
marginal valuation of the set of increments $(q_1 - q_0)$. Thus the
indifference tests tell us that the marginal valuation of the set of
increments lies between the values of the set at A-prices and at
B-prices; while the value of the set at A-prices is greater than
its value at B-prices. The latter is of course the same thing as
the first substitution theorem.

[1] See above, pp. 113–14.

Just as we deduced the Additivity of Compensating Variations in Income from the Transitivity of Indifference, so we can deduce the Additivity of Marginal Valuations. The marginal valuation of the increment from (q_0) to (q_2) equals the sum of the marginal valuations from (q_0) to (q_1) and from (q_1) to (q_2). This once established, we can proceed as before, breaking up the increment from (q_0) to (q_1) into a series of smaller increments—

taking, for example, one nth part of the total increment in each commodity to form a first set, a second nth part to compose a second set, and so on. Application of the indifference tests to these sub-increments will then narrow the gap between the limits of the whole marginal valuation, as it did in the corresponding place of 'price into quantity' theory. Thus if we here begin by taking an arbitrary length FG on a *horizontal* axis (Fig. 21) we can set up the rectangle $AFGM$ to represent $(p_0 \cdot q_1 - q_0)$ and the rectangle $NFGB$ to represent $(p_1 \cdot q_1 - q_0)$. Dividing up the increment of quantities, we get a generalized marginal valuation curve AB. The marginal valuation of the whole increment $(q_1 - q_0)$ is then represented

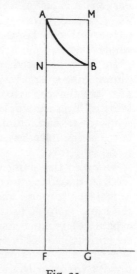

Fig. 21.

by the area $AFGB$, while the first substitution theorem is reflected in the downward slope of the curve AB.

In this sense, what the first substitution theorem becomes is nothing else but a generalized law of Diminishing Marginal Valuation. If the consumer acquires a set of increments of certain commodities at the maximum price which he is prepared to pay for that set of increments, his marginal valuation of a further (small) set of similar increments in the new position must be less than his marginal valuation of such a set of increments would have been in the old position. This is a recognizable generalization of the old 'Law of Diminishing Marginal Utility', though it has to be understood with a qualification that the old law omitted to emphasize. If we have seemed to take a step backward by inserting that qualification, we have been enabled thereby to take a considerable step forward in another way.

With all the history that lies behind us, I imagine that our law will go more easily by the name of diminishing marginal valuation than by its other name of first substitution theorem. But its statement as a substitution theorem remains the easier to grasp. Perhaps it is just as well that it should get its name from one of its faces and its definition from the other; for that is in accordance with the Janus-facedness which is characteristic of the whole theory.

In its generalized, as in its elementary, form, the law of diminishing marginal valuation only holds good as between positions that can actually be taken up on the market. The possibility of 'upward-sloping stretches' among positions which cannot be so taken up remains theoretically open here, just as it did in the elementary case. But there seems to be no more that needs to be said about it.

4. From this point we could go on, just as we did in Chapter XII, to deduce the reciprocity theorem. But there is no point in working through that argument again, for it will only give us the same reciprocity theorem, which (as we saw) is as directly capable of being taken over into valuation theory as the first substitution theorem or law of diminishing marginal valuation. We should however pause to make some examination of the reciprocity theorem from the new point of view; for though the theorem itself is the same from either aspect, the special case of the theorem, to which attention has mainly to be directed, is different.

The simplest case of the reciprocity theorem, from the other point of view, was that which established identity between the cross-effect of the price of X on the demand for Y and the cross-effect of the price of Y on the demand for X. For it was from this that we got the reciprocity of substitutes and complements. What we have now to consider are the cross-effects of quantities on prices (or marginal valuations). This is not the same problem as the other, since in the former case it was assumed that all prices other than those of X and Y remained constant; while in the new problem it will be proper to assume that the *quantities* of commodities other than X and Y remain constant (excepting of course the money commodity, the quantity of which must be allowed to vary so as to maintain indifference). What we have accordingly to do is to consider three positions A, B, C which are such that (1) the price of 'money' remains constant at unity throughout, (2) the quantity of money is varied so as to maintain indifference. From A to B the quantity of commodity X is increased, the quantities of all other commodities (including Y, but excluding money) remaining constant; the change in prices (maybe all the variable prices) is such as to bring about a change in quantities of this character. From A to C the quantity of commodity Y is increased, the quantities of all other commodities (including X, but excluding money) remaining constant; the change in prices being again that which is appropriate for this change in quantities. Then if, as we have done before, we write $A(q)$ at (p), $B(q+d_1 q)$ at $(p-d_1 p)$, $C(q+d_2 q)$ at $(p-d_2 p)$, the Reciprocity theorem gives $(d_1 p . d_2 q) = (d_2 p . d_1 q)$. Now the change in the quantity of money does not appear in either of these cross-sum-products, because the price of money is constant; all other terms (excepting that for Y) disappear from the cross-sum-product on the left, since $d_2 q$ is zero for all non-money commodities other than Y; all other terms (excepting that for X) disappear from the cross-sum-product on the right, since $d_1 q$ is zero for all non-money commodities other than X. Thus we are left with a Y-term on the left, and an X-term on the right. The Reciprocity theorem accordingly tells us that

$$d_1 p_y . d_2 q_y = d_2 p_x . d_1 q_x,$$

whence
$$d_1 p_y / d_1 q_x = d_2 p_x / d_2 q_y.$$

The change in the price of Y resulting from a unit change in the quantity of X equals the change in the price of X resulting from a unit change in the quantity of Y—the quantities of all other commodities than money being kept constant in each case, and the quantity of money being adjusted so as to maintain indifference.

Now this, it must be emphasized, is not the same as the corresponding result which we got previously. We have not merely taken the reciprocals of the fractions which we took when setting out that corresponding result; the *ceteris paribus* clauses are not the same. In the other case the prices of 'other' goods were held constant; in this case the quantities. Consequently, although the reciprocity theorem holds in either case, it is not the same relation between commodities which is shown to be reciprocal in the one case as in the other. Though we can usefully construct definitions of substitutes and complements which correspond to this new relation, they will not necessarily be equivalent to the old definitions. There are in fact two alternative definitions of substitution (complementarity), of which the former (which was discussed in Chapter XII) is the *Value and Capital* definition; while the latter, to which we have now come, is closer to that which was formerly presented, in terms of a cardinal theory, by Edgeworth and Pareto.

I propose to distinguish between these two definitions by saying that X and Y are p-substitutes when they are substitutes according to the former definition—a fall in the price of X diminishing the demand for Y, when all *prices* save that of X are fixed, and income is adjusted so as to maintain indifference. I shall say that X and Y are q-substitutes when a rise in the quantity of X diminishes the marginal valuation of Y (or the price at which a fixed quantity of Y would be purchased) when the *quantities* of all other commodities than X are fixed, saving the quantity of money, which is adjusted so as to maintain indifference. Similarly for p-complements and q-complements.[1]

If X and Y are p-substitutes, it does not necessarily follow that they are q-substitutes, nor vice versa. It is only in the simplest case that it will follow. Suppose that the prices of all commodities other than X and Y are fixed, so that we have effectively nothing more to deal with than a triad of goods, X, Y, and money. Since money is available to serve as a background commodity, X and Y may be p-substitutes or p-complements. Let us suppose that they are p-substitutes. Then a compensated fall in the price of X will increase the demand for X and diminish the demand for Y, while the price of Y remains fixed. In order

---

[1] The distinction between the two meanings of substitutes and complements was very clearly made by Dr. J. L. Mosak (op. cit., pp. 45–47). What I call p-substitutes he calls direct substitutes; my q-substitutes he calls inverse substitutes. Though I was at one time attracted by his terminology, I have finally decided against it; for I have come to feel that the one variety is no more direct (or inverse) than the other.

to offset this effect on the demand for Y, we must superimpose a fall in the price of Y. Now if there are falls in price for both X and Y, and they are such as to leave the quantity of Y demanded the same as it was initially, they must (by the substitution theorem) tend to increase the demand for X. Thus a situation in which the quantity of X increases, that of Y is constant, and that of money is adjusted to maintain indifference, is a situation in which the price of Y is reduced. Thus X and Y are q-substitutes.

In the same way, still working with the same triad, assume that X and Y are p-complements. A fall in the price of X will now cause the demand for Y to rise (the price of Y remaining constant). Thus if the demand for Y is to be kept constant, the price of Y must rise. Again, a fall in the price of X and a rise in that of Y, if it is to keep the demand for Y constant, must tend to increase the demand for X. Thus we have the situation which is expressed by saying that X and Y are q-complements.

Thus so long as the prices of all other goods than X and Y are fixed, the definitions of p- and q-substitutes and complements are exactly equivalent. But once the prices of additional goods are allowed to vary, this ceases to be true. For suppose that there are three goods with possibly variable prices (X, Y, Z) so that income is spent upon these three goods and money. Then if X and Y are p-complements, a compensated fall in the price of X will increase the demand for Y if the price of Z remains constant; we have seen that this implies that an increase in the quantity of X must increase the marginal valuation of Y (the price at which a given quantity of Y would be purchased) so long as the price of Z remains constant. But it is always possible that these changes might affect the demand for Z. If the price of Z is adjusted so as to keep the consumption of Z from changing, this may have a cross-effect on the demand for Y (at a fixed price of Y); it is entirely possible that this cross-effect may wipe out the initial increase in the demand for Y, so that after the price of Z is adjusted, the demand for Y will be diminished. If so, it will be a fall, rather than a rise, in the price of Y which will be needed in order to keep the demand for Y from changing. X and Y would be q-substitutes, even though they are p-complements.

It may not often happen that reactions through third goods

will cause p-complements to turn into q-substitutes, or p-substitutes into q-complements. But it is a thing which may happen on occasion. We do therefore need to make a distinction between the two meanings of the relationship. The reciprocity theorem holds for each of the two meanings, but the two meanings are not necessarily the same.

It must of course be emphasized that the reciprocity theorem between q-substitutes (and complements), like that between p-substitutes (and complements), is a property of indifferent positions; it may require modification if the additional units are acquired on terms which do not leave the consumer with that quantity of money which is needed to maintain indifference. We have however learned (in Chapter VIII above) the main things which need to be said about the effects on marginal valuations of changes in the quantity of 'money'. There is nothing new which needs to be added here.

5. Let us therefore turn to consider the remaining inversion, that of the second substitution theorem. Here it is proper to begin by observing that this theorem is itself something of a link between demand theory and valuation theory, or (as we may now permit ourselves to say) between p-theory and q-theory. For it will be remembered that the law of diminishing marginal valuations, and the reciprocity theorem between q-substitutes and q-complements, which we have derived by giving a q-interpretation of the general theorems, could also have been derived from the corresponding p-cases of the general theorems, by solving a set of simultaneous equations. But this alternative method of derivation, on which one may often be tempted to fall back, only gives the same result as the direct method, if the second substitution theorem (and its congeners of higher order) can be taken to be true. Thus we need these theorems in order to establish the internal consistency of the whole theory.

Suppose, for instance, that we have a triad of goods, X, Y, and 'money', which are such that the demands for X and Y depend linearly upon the prices of X and Y; thus

$$q_x = -ap_x + hp_y + g,$$
$$q_y = h'p_x - bp_y + f,$$

where $a, h, g, ...$, are constants. The law of demand tells us that

a, b are positive; the reciprocity theorem tells us that h, h' differ only by the income-effects contained in them. Now if we take q_x, q_y as independent variables, and solve for p_x, p_y, we get the inverted equations

$$(ab-hh')p_x = -bq_x-h'q_y'+g',$$
$$(ab-hh')p_y = -hq_x-aq_y+f',$$

where g', f', are again constants. Now these equations verify the conclusions derived from valuation theory, if (but only if)

$$ab-hh' \geqslant 0.$$

But since $ab-hh' = ab - \left(\dfrac{h+h'}{2}\right)^2 + \left(\dfrac{h-h'}{2}\right)^2,$

the necessary inequality follows at once from the second substitution theorem, in the form which we gave it when we had made allowance for income effects. We could similarly use the higher-order substitution theorems to verify the consistency of the theory for cases in which a larger number of commodities were in question.

If we write the inverted equations

$$p_x = -Aq_x-Hq_y+G,$$
$$p_y = -H'q_x-Bq_y+F,$$

the corresponding q-inequality, $AB-\left(\dfrac{H+H'}{2}\right)^2 \geqslant 0$, will now follow from the above; or it could be derived directly by the same process as that by which we established the corresponding p-theorem.

6. It is quite probable that the second substitution theorem is of more use in economics when it is expressed in this q-form than it is in its p-form; though the two are of course nothing more than alternative expressions of the same general theorem. The reader may first be reminded that the theory of the *working* of the General Equilibrium system under perfect competition (as expounded in *Value and Capital*, Chapter V) rests ultimately upon this proposition. I am, however, sure that this is by no means the only application which can be made of it. A brief indication of another, quite different, application will be a fitting way of concluding this chapter.

Suppose that we are studying the maximum-profit policy of a monopolist who is producing two products. The demands for the products are taken to be interdependent, but for small changes the amounts demanded are linearly dependent on the prices, so that the prices themselves are linearly dependent upon the outputs produced. The inverted equations, just written, may then be taken to represent the demand functions which confront our monopolist. The total revenue which he can expect is then

$$p_x q_x + p_y q_y = -Aq_x^2 - (H+H')q_x q_y - Bq_y^2 + Gq_x + Fq_y.$$

This, being a function of two variables, can be drawn out in the familiar 'indifference-curve' manner, with the two outputs plotted along two axes; it will be shown as a family of 'equal-revenue curves', each of which joins points which represent pairs of outputs giving equal revenue. Each of these curves will be a curve of the second degree. Its centre will be found at that pair of outputs which makes the marginal revenue of each product equal to zero. Assuming that this happens for some finite outputs, the curve must be an ellipse or a hyperbola. But the test which determines whether it is an ellipse or a hyperbola is nothing else than that with which we have just been concerned. If $AB > \left(\dfrac{H+H'}{2}\right)^2$, the curve must be an ellipse. It follows that the part of the curve in which we are interested (that over which the two marginal revenues are positive) must be convex to the axes, so that it will bend in the same way as the ordinary indifference curve. This will be true whether the two commodities are complements or substitutes.

The argument which has led to this conclusion is not sufficiently secure for us to be able to conclude that the curve will have this shape in every conceivable case. But it can be taken to establish that the elliptic form is the standard shape of the curve.

XVII

COMPLEMENTS AND SUBSTITUTES
FURTHER CONSIDERED

1. The point has now been reached where it becomes incumbent upon us to face up to a wide question, which was first brought to the attention of economists by Dr. Lange.[1]

Now that we have distinguished between p- and q-complements (and substitutes), it is all the more natural to ask whether there is not any way in which we can regard both varieties as particular manifestations of a more fundamental relationship. Such an interpretation is particularly inviting on the side of complements. When we try to think of examples of complements, we usually find ourselves thinking of commodities which have a tendency to be used together, pen and ink, petrol and lubricating oil, goods which are such that an increase in the consumption of Y *goes with* an increase in the consumption of X, whatever has been the cause which increased the consumption of X in the first place. In such instances, a change in the price of X is no more than a particular initiating cause, which reveals (as other causes may do equally) the intrinsic complementarity between the two goods. Other causes would operate in the same way. A change in income, for instance, would be such a cause. If X and Y are complements, in this deeper sense, we should expect that they would respond together to a change in income; both would be normal, or both inferior, not one normal and one inferior. Nor need we stop there; for at this point we need not be bound by the assumption of a fixed scale of preferences, which has been the basis of all our work up to the present. The close associations between groups of commodities, which we are now contemplating, should sometimes continue to be traceable even when there are changes in the system of wants. Thus the cause of the increase in X-consumption may lie right outside the price-system. If the consumption of petrol increases, because motoring

---

[1] O. Lange, 'Complementarity and Inter-relations of Shifts in Demand' (*Review of Economic Studies*, Oct. 1940).

has become more fashionable, it would be surprising if the consumption of lubricating oil did not similarly increase.

So far, we do not seem to have found any way of fitting 'intrinsic complementarity' of this sort into our theory of demand. I think it can be fitted in; but before explaining the way in which I now believe we should deal with it, it is desirable to examine an ingenious argument which appears at first sight to establish a direct relation between 'intrinsic complementarity' and the sorts of complementarity which we have hitherto discussed. This argument, which is due to Mr. Ichimura,[1] may be summarized, in our present terminology, in the following way.

2. Consider the position of a consumer who, as usual, is consuming quantities (q) at prices (p). Being in equilibrium, his marginal valuations of the goods which he is purchasing may be taken to be equal to these prices. Now suppose that this situation is disturbed, not by any change in prices or in income, but by a change in wants. This change in wants may be properly expressed, in accordance with what we have now established, by a change in the marginal valuations of the (q) quantities, from (p) to $(p+dp)$. Now a position in which market prices are (p) but marginal valuations are $(p+dp)$ is not an equilibrium position; the quantities (q) will need to be adjusted to $(q+dq)$ in order to be such as would be chosen, with the new system of wants, at prices (p). The effect on *consumption* of the change in wants is then the change in quantities from (q) to $(q+dq)$.

So far, we are doing no more than generalize Marshall, who showed an increase in the demand for a commodity as proceeding in two steps: (1) a vertical movement of the demand curve, due to a rise in marginal utility, or marginal valuation, (2) a movement along the new demand curve, adjusting quantity demanded so as to make marginal valuation equal to market price. What is important to notice is that the intermediate disequilibrium position, with quantities (q) and valuations $(p+dp)$, might itself have been an equilibrium position under appropriate market conditions. It would first of all have been necessary for prices to be adjusted so as to equal the new marginal valuations. But this would not, in general, be sufficient; for the

[1] S. Ichimura, 'A Critical Note on the Definition of Related Goods' (*Review of Economic Studies*, 1950–1).

value of the quantities (q) at $(p+dp)$ will not in general be the same as their value at (p). In order for it to be possible for the consumer to purchase quantities (q) at prices $(p+dp)$, income would have to be adjusted by the amount of the cost-difference $(dp.q)$. If prices were adjusted to $(p+dp)$, and income was adjusted by the amount of the cost-difference, the intermediate disequilibrium position would be made into an equilibrium position—at the new system of wants.

The course of adjustment may then be followed through in two steps. We begin with a situation in which the system of wants is of type A; quantities (q) are consumed at prices (p). We pass on to one in which wants have changed to type B, prices are adjusted to $(p+dp)$, and income to $(p+dp.q)$; in these conditions the same quantities (q) are consumed, in spite of the changes which have occurred. Thus at B_1 (as we may call this position), wants are of type B, but quantities (q) are still selected; B_1 has been made into an equilibrium position by the changes in prices and in income. Then, as a final step, we go back to the original prices (p), returning income to its original value $(p.q)$. The set of quantities $(q+dq)$ consumed in this final position (B_2) gives us the effect on consumption of the change in wants, prices and income being unchanged from what they were initially.

3. The simplest case of the analysis which is suggested by this construction is effectively Marshall's. Suppose that there is a change in the marginal valuation of one good only, and that we are only interested in the consumption of that good. The movement from A to B_1 can then be shown as the vertical shift of a demand curve;[1] the movement from A to B_2 is the horizontal shift in the same curve. But the movement from B_1 to B_2 is a movement *along* the new demand curve; it will be large or small according as that demand curve is elastic or inelastic. Thus there is a sense in which the effect of a shift in demand depends upon elasticity; if the vertical shift is (somehow) given, the extent of the horizontal shift depends on the elasticity of demand.

The same notion can be applied to more complicated cases. The next in sequence would be that in which the initial shift in

---

[1] Strictly speaking, it is not the Marshallian demand curve which is here in question, but one which is compensated for the cost-difference.

marginal valuation is still in respect of one commodity (X) only, but in which we are interested in the effect of that shift on the demand for another commodity (Y). Since the quantities of all commodities consumed are the same at B_1 as at A, the change in consumption of Y will be the same from A to B_2 as from B_1 to B_2. But the change from B_1 to B_2 is of a kind with which we have long been familiar; it is the result of a change in price combined with a change in income by the amount of the cost-difference (and no change in wants). Though the income-change is now equal to the cost-difference, not to the compensating variation, it will be approximately true to say that an initial rise in the marginal valuation of X (only) will cause the consumption of Y to expand if X and Y are p-complements, to contract if they are p-substitutes. Thus in the same sense as it is true that the effect of a shift in the marginal valuation of X on the consumption of X depends on the elasticity of demand for X, it is true that the effect on the consumption of Y depends on their p-substitutability or complementarity. To this extent it is possible to carry over the notions which are derived from indifference theory so as to deal with cases in which the system of wants does not remain constant.

This is a perfectly valid argument; but it does not help us as much as appears at first sight. We are helped to put it in its place if we observe that, like most arguments in demand theory, it is capable of inversion. Instead of regarding B_1 as a stage on the road to B_2, we can regard B_2 (or something like it) as a stage on the road to B_1. This is particularly evident in the Marshallian case, where we are interested in one commodity only. Instead of taking the vertical shift in the curve as given, and saying that the horizontal shift depends upon the elasticity of the curve, we can take the horizontal shift as given, and say that the vertical shift depends upon the elasticity. The Ichimura argument can be given a q-interpretation in exactly the same way.

As usual, we have to be a little careful about the passage from the p- to the q-form. It is important, in q-theory, to hold firm to a background of 'money'; it is only possible for the demand *for one commodity only* to be increased from A to B_2 if we take it to be implied that the demand for 'money' has diminished to a corresponding amount. Suppose, then, that B_2 quantities are

$(q_x+dq_x,\ q_y,\ m-dm)$; the quantity of X being increased from A to B_2, while q_y here stands for the unchanged quantities of all goods other than X and money. These quantities are taken with B-wants at p-prices. We proceed to ask what would be the marginal valuations of A quantities $(q_x,\ q_y,\ m)$ with B-wants. Once again, the movement from B_2 to this position B_1 may not be a movement between indifferent positions, though it is a movement from one position to another on the same scale of preferences. If we adjust the quantity of money to remove the income effect, we can say that the reduction in the quantity of X between B_2 and B_1 must raise its marginal valuation (as we have seen); and that the marginal valuation of another non-money commodity Y will be *lowered* if X and Y are q-complements, raised if X and Y are q-substitutes.

This gives us, if we put the p- and q-arguments together, the following result. If X and Y are both p-complements and q-complements, an increase in the marginal valuation of X only will be reflected in an increase in the quantities demanded of both X and Y; an increase in the quantity demanded of X only will correspond to a rise in the marginal valuation of X combined with a fall in the marginal valuation of Y. These conclusions are evidently consistent with one another. They can be combined in the statement that if X and Y are complements, from both the points of view of indifference theory, it is more likely that their quantities will move together, when there is a change in wants, than that their marginal valuations will do so. Even if marginal valuations move independently, the complementarity will tend to tie the quantities together. The fact that quantities move together will not necessarily imply that the marginal valuations are moving in the same direction.[1]

This is the result to which the Ichimura argument seems to lead; it is perfectly acceptable in itself, but it does not throw much light upon the nature of 'intrinsic complements'. For in the case of intrinsic complements, we should expect the marginal valuations to move together; it then follows by the Ichimura

---

[1] Similarly, if X and Y are close substitutes, it is more likely that their prices (or marginal valuations) will move together than that their quantities will do so. Perfect substitutes tend to have constant price-ratios, perfect complements constant quantity-ratios. It all fits in.

argument, that since such complements would also be *p*- and
q-complements, the quantities consumed would move together
a fortiori.[1] This is true; but in order to get more light on the
subject, we have to proceed, I now think, in another way.

4. What we have to do is to pick up a distinction which has
been nearly obliterated in the work of Pareto and his school but
which is quite at home in the theories of value that derive from
Menger.[2] Only a part of the inter-relatedness between the goods
which enter into a consumer's budget can properly be attributed
to characteristics of the consumer's wants or 'tastes'; there is a
part which has a technical character, being similar to the relations between the inputs which are combined in production.
The complementarity between petrol and oil to the private
motorist is of the same character (even, in a sense, of the same
economic character) as the complementarity between petrol and
oil to the bus company; we are asking for trouble if we treat
them too differently. It would accordingly appear that we ought
to think of the consumer as choosing, according to his preferences, between certain *objectives*; and then deciding, more or
less as the entrepreneur decides, between alternative *means* of
reaching those objectives. The commodities which he purchases
are for the most part means to the attainment of objectives, not
objectives themselves.[3]

So far as the greater part of the theory of demand is concerned,
a reformulation in these terms would not make much difference.
We could say, if we liked, that a reduction in the price of commodity X reduced the costs of those objectives for which X was
a means, and accordingly set up a tendency for these objectives

---

[1] Since I did not have these results when I wrote *Value and Capital*, there
are some passages in that book which make harder reading than they should
do, though I do not think that they are formally wrong. Thus I illustrated the
working of the price-system, in competitive conditions, by supposing an
increase in the quantity demanded of X only, while at the same time supposing that X and Y were *p*-complements. As we now see, this can happen; but
it cannot happen if X and Y are intrinsic complements, as my readers have
often (very naturally) supposed to be the case. I hope that this difficulty is
cleared up by what has been said in the present chapter.

[2] See, for instance, L. Robbins, *Nature and Significance of Economic
Science*, ch. 2.

[3] I owe the suggestion of this approach, partly to a conversation with Mr.
Ichimura himself, and partly to Mr. J. Faaland, of Nuffield College; each of
whom made the most useful comments on an earlier draft of this chapter.

to be substituted for others. It would also reduce the cost of much X-using methods of attaining these objectives relatively to the costs of less X-using methods; and would accordingly set up a tendency for these methods to be substituted for the others. (All this exactly analogously to the distinction between consumers' substitution and producers' substitution in the demand for factors of production.) But the total effect of the two substitutions together would obey the same rules as those which we have worked out without using this distinction. Thus, over the greater part of the field, it is a distinction which does not help very much.

But in the study of shifts in demand it is more to the point. Once we have drawn a distinction between means and objectives, we can distinguish between changes in wants which are due to a revaluation of objectives, and those which are due to changes in technique, in the technical methods by which objectives can be attained. Now if the prices of commodities remain constant, and there is an increase in the demand for a particular objective (relatively to others), it will tend to increase the demands for all those commodities which are currently required as means to that objective; they will accordingly behave as complements with respect to that shift in demand. These same commodities will behave as p-complements, if there is a fall in the price of one of them, and this change in price does not result in any change in technical method; all that then happens is that the objective to which the commodity contributes is substituted for other objectives, because its cost has fallen relatively to their costs. But it is entirely possible that a fall in the price of a particular commodity may induce a change in the method of attaining the particular objective for which it is used; in that case (as is the case of a factor of production) the commodities which would have been complements to it if the old method had been retained, may cease to be complements. Or there may be a 'shift in wants' which investigation shows to be the result of the introduction of a new method of utilization; this again may break the complementarity which persists only so long as old methods of utilization remain unchanged.

A complete theory of demand along these lines could be very complicated, especially when we consider the (frequent) cases of commodities which have more than one objective. Since the theory would be modelled on the theory of production, it could in principle be elaborated almost as far as the theory of production itself. Such complication is however no virtue; and it is a question how far it would be balanced by a simplification at what would be left of the 'consumption' end—namely the choice between the objectives themselves. If we could refine the objectives so far that there remained no complementarity between objectives (all of them being, as they would have to be, substitutes for each other), that would be a gain; but it is doubtful if we could go so far as that. And we could certainly not avoid the complication of 'inferiority' among objectives; the replacement of inferior by superior objectives would remain as a characteristic result of rising real income.

Finally, since the precise definition of these objectives would be, in practical cases, nearly impossible—and since the task of measuring their attainment, in any but the crudest of ways, looks quite unmanageable—their use can hardly be recommended as an instrument of applied economics or of econometric analysis. That is not their function; they are one of the visions which economists ought to see, now and then, if we are to be conscious of what it is that we are doing. If we remember that the consumer is himself, in his way, an entrepreneur, and that consumption has its problems of efficiency as well as production, we should do something to protect ourselves from one of the superficialities that are the diseases of our occupation.

XVIII

GENERALIZED CONSUMER'S SURPLUS

1. Only one thing now remains to be done, before we have completed the task of extending the elementary theory of Part II to the demand for a group of goods. This is the generalization of consumer's surplus, or rather of the whole set of related concepts which we have distinguished in that field. I do not pretend that this is a very important undertaking, or that the results which emerge from it have an intrinsic importance which is worth the trouble of getting them. But they do have some interest; and the inquiry is in any case one which ought not to be omitted. For if our general approach is sound, an investigation of this sort should be capable of being carried through; to show that it can be carried through provides a fairly searching test of the methods which we have been elaborating in this book.[1]

As we saw in Chapter X, the notion of consumer's surplus arises out of the application of valuation methods to the 'price into quantity' effects of a price-change with income constant; thus it only makes sense if it is applied to a situation which can be analysed from both points of view. This means that the generalization for which we are looking cannot be more than a limited generalization. Though we can deal with the case of a multiple price-change, in the sense of a change in the prices of several commodities, we cannot extend the analysis to the most general case, in which all prices vary. There must always be a sufficient background of fixed-price commodities, to serve as 'money'. Unless we have a sufficient 'money', we lack a suitable medium in which consumer's surplus can be measured.

Let us then begin, as we did in the elementary theory, by considering the effect of a particular *change* in prices (income being

---

[1] Autobiographically, as explained in the *preface*, it was through my first wrestlings with this problem that I became convinced of the desirability of reworking the whole theory of demand by the present approach.

constant); let us seek to identify the compensating variation in income and the (compensating) increment of consumer's surplus which are to be associated with the change. In the elementary theory, it was only one price that was changing, and here it is to be a group of prices; but we still distinguish between the price-changing commodities and the fixed-price commodities, which are lumped together to form 'money' or M. Let us then write (q) for the initial set of price-changing commodities only, while m is the initial quantity of M. The initial prices of the price-changing commodities may similarly be written (p), while the price of M is taken as unity. The initial situation may accordingly be denoted by

(A) (q, m) quantities at $(p, 1)$ prices,

while after the price-change (without change in income) the consumer will be taking

(B) $(q+dq, m+dm)$ quantities at $(p-dp, 1)$ prices.

As in the elementary theory, we have then to construct intermediate positions b and β, from which we derive the compensating variation and the consumer's surplus respectively. b and β are each of them indifferent with A; b is such that it would be selected at B-prices and some suitable income, the compensating variation (C) being the difference between A-income and b-income; β is such that β-quantities are $(q+dq, m+dm-c)$. Thus β contains the same quantities of all goods as B, except that the quantity of M is diminished by c (the increment of consumer's surplus). These are the natural generalizations of our 'elementary' definitions when several prices are changing.

2. In the elementary theory, we were able to exhibit all these magnitudes on a diagram, and from the diagram their mutual relations could be read off. Here also it will be convenient to begin by examining how far we can proceed by diagrammatic methods; for it has already become apparent that geometrical analysis can take us some way, even when we are dealing with multiple changes in prices and consumption.

Let us accordingly start off, more or less as we did in Chapter XIII, by taking an arbitrary length HK on a vertical axis (Fig. 22). Let us construct rectangles $HANK$, $HMBK$ on it to represent the cost-differences L and P, which are $(dp.q)$ and $(dp.q+dq)$ respectively. Their difference $(dp.dq)$ is accordingly represented by the rectangle $AMBN$. Now, using AM as base, construct a rectangle $AFGM$ to represent $(p.dq)$—the value of the increment (dq) at A-prices. It follows, by subtraction, that the rectangle $NFGB$ represents $(p-dp.dq)$—the value of the increment (dq) at B-prices. All these areas can accordingly be

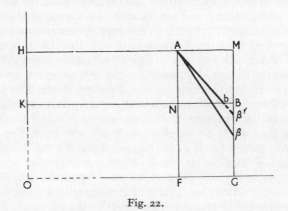

Fig. 22.

given exactly the same significance as they had on the one-commodity diagram.

So far, so good; but this is a diagram which must be used with much care. What we cannot do in this case, as of course we could do in the one-commodity case, is to complete the figure, so as to treat HK and FG as a pair of axes, meeting in the usual way at O. At least, if we do so, we must recognize that the areas so shown do not have their usual significance. $OHAF$ does not, in general, represent $(p.q)$; for if it did so, we should have

$$\frac{(dp.q)}{(p.q)} = \frac{\text{rect. } HANK}{\text{rect. } OHAF} = \frac{HK}{OH} = \frac{\text{rect. } ANBM}{\text{rect. } AFGM} = \frac{(dp.dq)}{(p.dq)},$$

and these ratios of sum-products, though they are necessarily equal in the one-commodity case, are not by any means necessarily equal in the general case.[1] We must therefore rest content with our truncated diagram.

There is however no reason why we should not make use of it as far as it will take us. We can still construct a point b on KB, so that the strip $HAbK$ represents (in the usual way) the compensating variation; and we can construct a point β on BG, so that the strip $AFG\beta$ represents the marginal valuation of the increment (dq). These constructions are no more than we have performed, and justified, in Figs. 19 and 21 respectively.[2] But here again these constructions tell us less than the corresponding constructions told us in the elementary theory. For the compensated demand curve Ab and the marginal valuation curve $A\beta$ have now been constructed by quite distinct and separate processes; we have no right to assume identity between them. The relation between them will have to be investigated by other methods.

Some of the propositions which we established in the elementary theory can however be seen at once, from Fig. 22, to hold quite generally. If C is the compensating variation in income, then $C \geqslant L$ (as we already know); it follows at once from the downward slope of the compensated demand curve Ab. If c is the (compensating) increment of consumer's surplus, which is measured (as in the elementary theory) by the rectangle $HANK$ plus the difference between the strip $AFG\beta$ and the rectangle $NFGB$, it follows from the downward slope of the marginal valuation curve that $c \leqslant P$. These results do appear from our diagram; but in order to go farther we have to make a different approach.

---

[1] This can readily be verified for the case where there are just two goods whose prices are changing. The above ratios will then only be equal if the two prices are changing in the same proportion or if the two quantities are changing in the same proportion; in either case the two goods would be such that they could be treated, for present purposes, as a single commodity.

In general, it is not even necessary that $(p.dq)$ should be positive when $(dp.q)$ is positive, though I have drawn the diagram for the case in which that is so. In the case when these two magnitudes had opposite signs, it would be necessary to displace one of the axes (as was done, for the study of the effects of the price-change, in Fig. 20 on p. 124 above). But this displacement would not affect the essential part of the diagram—the rectangle $ANBM$, and the points b, β, and β'—which would remain as shown.

[2] I have drawn Fig. 22 for the normal case, in which the income effect is positive; the construction of the corresponding diagram for the 'inferior' case is left to the reader.

3. Analytically, the two propositions which we have so far verified are consequences of the indifference tests as between the indifferent positions A and b, and A and β respectively. But we are here operating with *three* indifferent positions; and from the indifference of three positions more than these two results can be extracted. We can, in the first place, apply the indifference tests to the pair b and β. b is the chosen position at b-prices (which are the same as B-prices); it follows that the value of b-quantities at b-prices cannot exceed the value of β-quantities at b-prices. (In these values the quantities of M must of course be reckoned.) Now the value of b-quantities at b-prices equals initial income less the compensating variation in income; while, since β contains the same quantity of all goods as B, except that the amount of m is diminished by c, the value of β-quantities at B-prices equals final income less the increment of consumer's surplus. Since income is unchanged between A and B, the indifference test tells us that $-C \leqslant -c$; or $c \leqslant C$. This is the third main inequality of the elementary theory, which has accordingly been shown to be valid generally, though not by the geometrical method.

4. This is clearly as far as we can go without making linearity assumptions; before we look to see what further we can get from such assumptions, it will be well to rewrite our inequalities in the form which we know to be appropriate as soon as the curves Ab, $A\beta$ are treated as straight lines.

The substitution effect of the price-change is now measured by the rectangle with base Nb and height HK; the income effect by the rectangle with base bB and height HK. We call these S and I respectively. Then, as usual, we have

$$P-L = (dp \,.\, dq) = S+I; \qquad C = L + \tfrac{1}{2}S.$$

Our first inequality reduces to the substitution theorem between A and b $(S \geqslant 0)$.

We are now unable to express the substitution and income effects on the valuation side directly in terms of S and I, as we could do in the elementary theory. The substitution effect on marginal valuation is however measured by the rectangle with base FG and height $M\beta$, the income effect by the rectangle with base FG and height $B\beta$. Let us call these s and i. (It will be remembered that the income effect on marginal valuation goes the opposite way from the income effect on demand.) Thus we have here

$$P-L = (dp \cdot dq) = s-i; \qquad c = P-\tfrac{1}{2}s.$$

Our second inequality $(c \leqslant P)$ reduces to the substitution theorem between A and β $(s \geqslant 0)$.

Alternatively, we may express both C and c in terms of the 'Marshall measure' (M) which is the mean between L and P. Since $L = M-\tfrac{1}{2}(S+I)$, $C = M-\tfrac{1}{2}I$. Since $P = M+\tfrac{1}{2}(s-i)$, $c = M-\tfrac{1}{2}i$. Our third inequality, $c \leqslant C$, can therefore be written in the form $i \geqslant I$. The income-effect on marginal valuation tends to be greater than the income-effect on quantity demanded, when both take their origin from the same change in prices.

Put in this form, the conclusion at which we have just arrived looks rather impressive—until we remember that exactly the same result was valid in the case of a change in the price of a single commodity. And we did not then have to stress this particular relation because it was arithmetically obvious. We could there prove that $i = I + \dfrac{I^2}{S}$, so that $i \geqslant I$ followed arithmetically from $S \geqslant 0$. What has happened to that formula in the present setting?

We can track it down if we turn to the links between *three* indifferent positions which we have not yet used. These are the reciprocity theorem and the second substitution theorem.

Let us write the actual quantities taken at b as

$$(q+d_1 q, \ m+d_1 m).$$

Let us construct prices $(p-d_2 p, 1)$ which are such that β-quantities would be taken at those prices, income being adjusted in such a way as to make these β-quantities just purchasable. Then our three indifferent positions are

$$A(q, m) \text{ at prices } (p, 1),$$
$$b(q+d_1 q, \ m+d_1 m) \text{ at prices } (p-dp, 1),$$
$$\beta(q+dq, \ m+dm-c) \text{ at prices } (p-d_2 p, 1).$$

In terms of this notation, we have $S+I = (dp \cdot dq)$, $S = (dp \cdot dq_1)$, and (assuming linearity of the marginal valuation curve) $s = (d_2 p \cdot dq)$.

Now the reciprocity theorem, between the three indifferent positions, tells us that $(d_2 p \cdot d_1 q) = (dp \cdot dq)$, so that $(d_2 p \cdot d_1 q)$ is also equal to $S+I$.

If only one price is changing, each of these sum-products becomes a simple product, and it is then obvious that

$$dp \cdot d_1 q \cdot d_2 p \cdot dq = d_2 p \cdot d_1 q \cdot dp \cdot dq,$$

so that $Ss = (S+I)^2$, whence $S(i+S+I) = (S+I)^2$, or

$$i = I + \frac{I^2}{S}.$$

In general, however, we know no more than that

$$(dp \cdot d_1 q)(d_2 p \cdot dq) \geqslant (d_2 p \cdot d_1 q)(dp \cdot dq),$$

which is the second substitution theorem. Accordingly (within the limits of that theorem's validity) we have $Ss \geqslant (S+I)^2$, or

$$i \geqslant I + \frac{I^2}{S}.$$

The equation is replaced by an inequality, but it is one from which the other inequality $(i \geqslant I)$ still follows at once.

Let us go back to our diagram, on which the line Ab has been extended to meet $B\beta$ at β'. The triangle $A\beta B$ has the area $\frac{1}{2}i$ (since its base is $B\beta$ and its height BN). The triangle $A\beta'B$ has the area

$$\frac{1}{2}\left(I + \frac{I^2}{S}\right)$$

as was shown geometrically in Chapter X. Thus it follows from our inequality that β lies below β', or that the line $A\beta$ slopes downwards more steeply than Ab. Though, when only one price is changing, the marginal valuation curve and the compensated demand curve are identical, there is a tendency, in the general case, for the (generalized) marginal valuation curve to slope downwards more steeply than the (generalized) compensated demand curve. At least this is so over stretches which are such that each curve can be treated as a straight line.

Now this is not a mere piece of geometry; it does appear to have some economic meaning. Both along Ab and $A\beta$ the consumer is moving from one indifferent position to another; he is keeping on the same 'indifference level' along both curves. But along Ab prices are moving by degrees towards their new position; and at each adjustment of prices the consumer is selecting that combination of increments of the various commodities which he prefers. At each stage he pays so much for the whole combination of increments that he is prevented from bettering his position; but so far as the composition is concerned, he selects whatever composition suits him best. Along $A\beta$, on the other hand, the combination of increments is imposed, as it were, from outside; it is regulated in such a way as to aim at a particular final collection of commodities, which (from the point of view of the step-by-step process) is an arbitrary collection. It is in accordance with general principles of demand theory that when the composition of the successive 'bundles' can be freely selected, the marginal valuations of the successive bundles should fall more slowly than they would do if this freedom did not exist. This,. I think, is the conclusion to which we have arrived; in these terms the whole theory seems to tie up, as it should do.[1]

5. It is now time to confront the obvious question: what, if anything, which is of practical importance emerges from all these symbols and diagrams? It is certainly not to be supposed that most of the magnitudes we have been discussing in this chapter could be identified in any practical instance; so far as the theory has any application, it is not a direct application of that character. I think, however, that the theory does have some indirect significance, which comes out clearly when we consider it in relation to the Marshallian argument, out of which it all sprang.

Marshall gave (1) a definition of consumer's surplus—the difference between what the consumer is willing to pay and what he does pay; and (2) a theorem, which measured consumer's surplus by the area under the demand curve. I do not think that Marshall himself maintained that this measure was more than an approximation; but he did hold—and I think our analysis

---

[1] I have not thought it necessary to cumber the above argument with Equivalent Variations and Surpluses. Obviously it can be put into reverse, proceeding from B to A, just as we put the one-commodity theory into reverse in Chapter X.

has confirmed his belief—that there are cases in which it is as good an approximation as we are likely to want. I myself would go so far as to say that in other cases, when the Marshall measure ceases to be a good approximation, there is little to be made of the concept itself; no useful conclusions can be drawn with its assistance. But in those cases in which the Marshall measure is a good measure, the concept is a useful concept; whether or not we are able to quantify it econometrically, it remains at the least an exceedingly convenient way of fixing the ideas.

What, in the light of this approach, we have been trying to do is to establish, more precisely than Marshall thought necessary, the conditions needed for the Marshall measure to be a good measure. And, so considered, the result of our inquiry is very simple. In order that the Marshall measure of consumer's surplus should be a good measure, one thing alone is needful—that the income effect should be small. Though this is itself a statement that can be interpreted in different senses, so that it is again a tricky matter to apply it directly, the theory also provides an alternative criterion, which is easier to grasp.

If the income effect (however defined) is not small, we do not merely get a significant divergence between the Marshall definition and the Marshall measure; from the definition there sprouts a family of related concepts, which may easily be mistaken for one another. We may begin by thinking of consumer's surplus as the maximum amount of money which the consumer, in the A-situation, would pay for a ticket entitling him to buy certain commodities at B-prices; but we now need to distinguish between a ticket which entitles him to buy the exact quantities which he would have bought if he had not had to pay for his ticket, and one which allows him to purchase any quantity he likes. The money he would pay for the former is the compensating consumer's surplus; what he would pay for the latter is the compensating variation in income. We have further to distinguish from these the money which he would accept for the one sort of ticket or the other, if he had been given it free, and was to be persuaded to return it. These are the equivalent consumer's surplus and equivalent variation in income.

In general, the Marshall measure does not fit any of these four concepts exactly; but it lies between the compensating and equivalent magnitudes—of either sort. Thus if the money which he would pay for the ticket, if he had not got it, and the money which he would accept in 'exchange for the ticket, if he had it already, are much the same, compensating and equivalent will fall together, and the Marshall measure will be a good measure of either. If we judge that the difference between the two surpluses is not great, the Marshall measure can be employed, and the theory has such usefulness as it is capable of possessing. But if we are bound to judge that there will be a serious divergence between them, the Marshall measure will do no more than give us a kind of mean, and that may help very little.

All this, we have learned in the present chapter, is equally valid whether the ticket gives the right of purchasing one commodity only, or whether it gives a right that is concerned with several commodities. But something remains to be said about the meaning of the Marshall measure in the more general case.

Let us look at Marshall's own application, in which the ticket gives entitlement to the acquisition, at a fixed price, of a commodity not otherwise available. Only suppose that it gives entitlement to the acquisition of two such commodities, which we will take to be close substitutes, say gas and electricity. Then the natural extension of Marshall's procedure is the following. We begin by constructing a demand curve for gas, on the assumption that electricity is not available; the surplus derived from the introduction of gas would be read off by taking the Marshall triangle under this curve. Let us call this triangle G_0. We next construct a demand curve for electricity, on the assumption that gas is already available at its fixed price; the surplus derived from the *additional* availability of electricity would again be read off by taking the Marshall triangle. Call that triangle E_1. Then the total surplus derived from the availability of both commodities would be $G_0 + E_1$.

It was, however, an arbitrary decision to begin with gas. We might equally have begun by taking the Marshall triangle from a demand curve for electricity with gas absent (E_0), and followed by taking that from a demand curve for gas with electricity available at its fixed price (G_1). The two commodities being close substitutes, E_0 would be much larger than E_1, and G_0 than G_1. These differences should, we may suppose, roughly balance.

But if the theory is to be coherent, we should get exactly the same result from either route, so that the differences should balance exactly. How do we know that they do that? In general, if we are working from Marshallian demand curves, and income effects are not negligible, there is no reason why they should balance exactly; that is one reason why the theory gets into trouble in such circumstances. But if the income effects are negligible, the triangles are good measures of the compensating variations in income; and we know (from the transitivity of indifference) that compensating variations are additive. Thus when income effects are negligible, so that the Marshallian analysis is applicable, we get the same result whether we take gas or electricity first. By either route we get an intelligible measure of consumer's surplus.

Thus the application to a group of commodities does not in itself endanger the surplus analysis. Yet it must be granted that we shall more often desire to select a group, than a single commodity, in such a way that the total income effect will be substantial; so that the four concepts of surplus are more likely to fly apart, and the technique of surplus analysis is more likely to break down.

XIX

THE INDEX-NUMBER THEOREM

1. All our analysis hitherto has been, in a sense (often, it is true, a much extended sense) Partial Analysis. In Part II we considered the demand for one commodity in terms of the rest. In Part III we have so far been considering the demand for a group of commodities in terms of the rest; it has indeed become increasingly clear, as we went on, that the scope of our investigations has been limited to that problem, and that alone. Nevertheless it is not quite true that demand theory is inherently so limited; we have caused it to be limited in that way by a particular step which we took at one stage of our discussion. There is something to be said about the Demand for All Commodities; there are certain problems in which we want to consider the structure of demand for all commodities, not (at least on the surface) in terms of anything else, not even 'money'. These are the problems of Index Numbers.

If A and B are indifferent, we have *two* inequalities between combinations of their p's and q's—the *two* indifference tests. Each of these tests, taken by itself, is asymmetrical; it gives us a view of the A-position from the B-position, or vice versa; in order to get a symmetrical relation between the two positions we have to combine the tests in some way. So far, we have always combined them in one way, which may be called 'adding' them; it is this which gave us the first substitution theorem, and all that has followed so far may be regarded as the development of that theorem. But we do start from two tests; if we only combine them in one way, we are losing something; it should be possible to combine them in another way in order to get a significant, symmetrical, result. It is possible to do this; instead of 'adding' them, we may 'multiply' them. It is the consequences of such 'multiplication' which will be considered in this chapter.

The process of 'addition' had the particular virtue that it caused all commodities whose prices did not change between A and B, or whose quantities did not change between A and B, to cancel out. The process of 'multiplication' does not have this virtue. Thus the results of multiplication are only interesting if we are prepared to consider, or to think that we are considering, the quantities and prices of all the commodities in the consumer's budget. That is what we endeavour to do, at least in principle, when we construct index-numbers (of prices or of quantities). That is why this particular method of combination has a special relevance to this field.

The positions which we compare, by the use of index-numbers, are ordinarily not indifferent positions; and they relate to the behaviour of groups, not to the behaviour of the individual consumer. The same was however true of our more sectional analysis. We can proceed here in the same way as we proceeded formerly. We can establish, in the first place, a proposition (corresponding to the first substitution theorem) which holds when a single consumer is moving from one indifferent position to another. We can then examine how far this proposition will continue to be true, if it is applied to positions which are not indifferent. Finally we can inquire how far it is applicable to the behaviour of a group of consumers, or ultimately, that is, to the economy as a whole.

2. q's and p's now refer to all commodities; we have no Marshallian 'money'. If A, being (q_0) at (p_0), and B, being (q_1) at (p_1), are indifferent, the indifference tests tell us that

$$(p_0 \cdot q_0) \leqslant (p_0 \cdot q_1) \quad \text{and} \quad (p_1 \cdot q_1) \leqslant (p_1 \cdot q_0).$$

All of these sum-products being positive, it follows that

$$(p_0 \cdot q_1)(p_1 \cdot q_0) \geqslant (p_0 \cdot q_0)(p_1 \cdot q_1).$$

This is the inequality which I call the Index-Number Theorem.

It merits its name for the following reason. Dividing through by $(p_0 \cdot q_0)(p_1 \cdot q_0)$, it becomes

$$\frac{(p_0 \cdot q_1)}{(p_0 \cdot q_0)} \geqslant \frac{(p_1 \cdot q_1)}{(p_1 \cdot q_0)}.$$

The first of these is the Laspeyre index of B-quant ties to base A; the second is the Paasche index. Thus the Laspeyre quantity-index tends to be greater than the Paasche quantity-index. If we similarly divide through by $(p_0 \cdot q_0)(p_0 \cdot q_1)$, we get

$$\frac{(p_1 \cdot q_0)}{(p_0 \cdot q_0)} \geqslant \frac{(p_1 \cdot q_1)}{(p_0 \cdot q_1)}.$$

The Laspeyre price-index tends to be greater than the Paasche price-index. Thus, as is well known, the same inequality holds, both for the quantity-index and for the price-index. We can work in terms of whichever we choose, for there is the same duality of q- and p-theory in this field as in other departments of demand theory. But it is unnecessary to repeat the argument in both forms, for conversion from the one form to the other is now automatic. I shall here work in terms of the quantity-index.

Let us then write **L** and **P** for the quantity-indexes. If A, B are indifferent, we may write

$$\mathbf{L} - \mathbf{P} = \mathbf{S}$$

and **S** may be regarded as a kind of substitution effect. The index-number theorem is itself a kind of substitution theorem, which may be expressed in the form $\mathbf{S} \geqslant 0$, analogously with the substitution effect to which we are accustomed.[1]

3. If A and B are not indifferent, we may, as usual, divide the whole movement into a substitution effect and an income effect. Let us here select an intermediate position a, which is indifferent to B, though it could be chosen at A-prices, if income were suitable. If $(q_0 + \delta q)$ are the a-quantities, while we write $(q_0 + \delta q + dq)$ for (q_1), we have

$$\mathbf{L} - \mathbf{P} = \frac{(p_0 \cdot q_1)}{(p_0 \cdot q_0)} - \frac{(p_1 \cdot q_1)}{(p_1 \cdot q_0)} = \frac{(p_0 \cdot \delta q + dq)}{(p_0 \cdot q_0)} - \frac{(p_1 \cdot \delta q + dq)}{(p_1 \cdot q_0)}$$

$$= \left[\frac{(p_0 \cdot \delta q)}{(p_0 \cdot q_0)} - \frac{(p_1 \cdot \delta q)}{(p_1 \cdot q_0)}\right] + \left[\frac{(p_0 \cdot dq)}{(p_0 \cdot q_0)} - \frac{(p_1 \cdot dq)}{(p_1 \cdot q_0)}\right] = \mathbf{I} + \mathbf{S}.$$

S refers to a movement between two indifferent positions and

---

[1] That here $\mathbf{L} \geqslant \mathbf{P}$, whereas in the partial p-theory $P \geqslant L$, is of course due to the convention, which we there adopted, of treating a *fall* in price as positive. If we had not adopted that convention, which did seem to make things easier for the time being, we should have had $L \geqslant P$ in all forms.

therefore tends to be positive. The index-number theorem will accordingly continue to hold, even as between non-indifferent positions, so long as the income-effect **I** is positive—or, if it is negative, so long as it is not so large as to outweigh the substitution effect.

The δq's are now the changes in consumption due to the change in real income. Let us write k_0 for the proportion of initial expenditure which was devoted to a particular commodity —so that $k_{0x} = p_{0x} q_{0x}/(p_0 \cdot q_0)$; let us similarly write k_1 for the proportion of expenditure which would have been devoted to that commodity if A-quantities had been purchased at B-prices —so that $k_{1x} = p_{1x} q_{0x}/(p_1 \cdot q_0)$. Then

$$\mathbf{I} = \left(k_0 - k_1 \cdot \frac{\delta q}{q} \right)$$

summed, of course, over all commodities. Since $\sum k_0$ (over all commodities) is unity, and $\sum k_1$ (over all commodities) is unity, **I** would be zero if the income-elasticities of all commodities were the same. **I** would also be zero if the set of k_1's was identical with the set of k_0's, as they would be if all prices had changed, from A to B, in the same proportion. **I** will be positive if the change in real income induces a relative expansion in the demands for those goods whose prices have relatively fallen; in this case, obviously, the income effect reinforces the substitution effect. **I** will be negative if the change in real income induces a relative expansion in demand for those goods whose prices have relatively risen. This is what has to happen if the income effect is to work against the substitution effect; a strong effect of this kind is what is needed if the index-number theorem, applied to non-indifferent positions, is to break down.

4. So far we have been considering the single consumer; let us now consider the body of consumers as a whole. We must now take an intermediate position a, which is such that each consumer would purchase his a-quantities at A-prices, when his income had been so adjusted as to keep his a-position indifferent with his B-position. By this means, the difference between **L** and **P**, taken over the whole body of consumers, can be analysed into an **S** and an **I**, each of which is taken over the whole body of consumers. The global **S** is a weighted average of individual

S's (the weights being positive), so that it must tend to be positive. The global **I** will again be transformable into the form

$$\left(k_0-k_1\cdot\frac{\delta q}{q}\right),$$

each of the component terms being now interpreted with reference to the body of consumers as a whole. Thus it is still true that the index-number law only breaks down if the change in real income induces a relative expansion in the demands for those goods whose prices have relatively risen. The only qualification which has to be added is that the change in real income must now cover a possible change in the distribution of real incomes, as well as a change in the average level of real income over the economy as a whole.

Substantially, then, there is only one type of exception to the index-number law, while to the generalized law of demand, which we examined in Chapter XV above, there were (as will be remembered) three possible types of exception. The law of demand, when applied to a group of commodities, the prices of which might change in any manner, could break down (1) because the group of commodities, taken as a whole, was inferior—the Giffen case, (2) because, when some prices were rising and some falling, the income effect tended to increase the demand for those goods whose prices were rising, relatively to the demand for those goods whose prices were falling, (3) because a change in the distribution of real income had a similar effect. Here, in our analysis of the index-number problem, we are not concerned with a particular group of commodities, but with all commodities; it is this which simplifies the result which we get. All commodities cannot be inferior; for that reason the first cause of exception drops out. Further, the fact that we are now only interested in relative prices makes it easier to amalgamate the second and third causes of exception. Otherwise, the two theories are exactly parallel.

5. They are indeed so exactly parallel that one is led to ask whether there is not some sense in which the one is a special case of the other. I believe that there is such a sense; it can be explained in the following way.

Let us suppose, for this particular purpose, that all commodities are finely divisible. Then suppose that each of the quantities of goods $(q_{0x}, q_{0y}, \ldots)$ composing (q_0) is divided into a large number (say n) equal parts, and that a 'bundle' or 'bale' is put together, consisting of one part of each commodity; call this an A-bundle. Similarly divide the (q_1) quantities into n equal parts, and put together a B-bundle. Consumption at A then consists of n A-bundles, and no B-bundles; consumption at B of n B-bundles, and no A-bundles. The consumer may be thought of as choosing between A-bundles and B-bundles; of course he has many other alternatives open to him, but a choice between buying A-bundles and buying B-bundles is one of the alternatives which is open. Now, looking at his demand for B-bundles, it expands from o to n as he moves from A to B; consequently, if the law of demand (in the sense we have used that term previously to this chapter) is to be valid, the price of B-bundles, in terms of the alternative (A-bundles) must have fallen. But, at A, the price of a B-bundle is $\frac{1}{n}(p_0 \cdot q_1)$; the price of an A-bundle is $\frac{1}{n}(p_0 \cdot q_0)$; thus the price of a B-bundle in terms of A-bundles is $(p_0 \cdot q_1)/(p_0 \cdot q_0)$, which is the Laspeyre quantity-index. Similarly, at B, the price of a B-bundle in terms of A-bundles is the Paasche quantity-index. The law of demand indicates that this price must have tended to fall from A to B, so that $\mathbf{L} \geqslant \mathbf{P}$. Thus the index-number theorem is a special case of the law of demand, after all.

I do not think that we ought to rely upon this argument as a proof of the index-number theorem, since it assumes a general divisibility, which it is better not to have to assume. Nevertheless I think it will be agreed that it throws an interesting light upon the nature of the comparisons which we have been making in this chapter. And the method of analysis which it employs is one that seems to be capable of extended application in other connexions which lie outside our present scope.

6. What does need to be said, in order to complete our present inquiry, is a word about its application. The index-number theorem does beyond question provide a test that can be applied to actual figures; but in applying it we should be clear about its significance. It is no more and no less than a test of the prefer-

ence hypothesis. If, for a moment, we put the *exception* on one side, we can say that if a body of consumers is behaving, over time, broadly in the way that a body of ideal consumers should be expected to behave, they must show $L \geqslant P$; for this inequality is a natural property of the reaction of unchanging wants to changing environment. If P exceeds L (the excess being sufficient to be significant statistically), then there is a presumption that wants have changed, so that a comparison between the two positions, with reference to an unchanging system of wants, cannot be made.

In spite of the *exception*, this conclusion remains, I believe, usually valid. Nevertheless the exception is not a mere theoretical curiosum, like the Giffen case; it is a real, and may be a serious, complication. It is indeed true that the multiplicity of commodities, and the multiplicity of the supply-and-demand forces acting upon them, do give us some reason to expect that the income-effect on the index-numbers will be small; if the changes in demand due to changes in real income are quite uncorrelated with price-changes, some of the components of I will go in one direction, some in the other, so that on balance they may largely cancel out. Over the whole range of commodities we should not, I think, expect to find a high correlation; but there may be some correlation, and it may go in a perverse direction. A case in which I would be large and negative is not hard to construct; and some of the conditions which are necessary for it are conditions that do evidently occur in some practical cases.

Consider the case of an 'underdeveloped' country which is endeavouring to industrialize, and which does succeed in reducing the real costs of production of a number of manufactured goods. It may, however, have no comparable success, or even no success at all, in increasing the supply of food. Then the main change in relative prices is a fall in the prices of manufactured goods relatively to those of foodstuffs; but these two classes of products are weak substitutes for one another, so that the substitution effect, due to this change in relative prices, may well be small. The increase in production nevertheless tends to lead to a rise in incomes. But the poor inhabitants of this country desire to spend an increase in incomes on more foodstuffs; they are

relatively uninterested in an increased consumption of manufactured commodities. In this case, which is not (in essentials) of an
altogether unfamiliar character, many of the conditions for an
exception would seem to be present. The substitution effect is
weak, and the income effect tends to go in a perverse direction.
There are, however, one or two points about this model which
merit attention.

In the first place, if the costs of manufactured goods (more of
which are not demanded) have fallen, while the costs of foodstuffs (more of which are easily demanded) have not fallen, the
'natural' reaction to the change is a movement of labour from
industry into food production. If equilibrium is restored in this
way, the conditions for our exceptional case are very likely to be
present. On the other hand, if the marginal product of labour in
agriculture is sharply falling, this movement will soon be brought
to a stop; but a concomitant of this must be the emergence of
large profits or rents in agriculture, and it would be surprising if
some of these did not get spent upon the products of industry.
This, however, is a normal income effect, which would tend to
counteract any perverse tendencies which had developed along
the first channel. In practice, however, in the modern instances
which will be in mind, it is evident that neither of these things
tends, very much, to happen; but that is surely because they are
prevented from happening. Manufacturing production is deliberately canalized in the direction of investment goods and of
public goods. In order to contrive this redirection, consumers'
expenditure has to be deliberately restricted, by taxation or
some other equivalent means. As a net result, the expansion in
consumers' real income (in any sense which is relevant to consumers' expenditure) is kept within narrow bounds. But if there
is no expansion in net income, there is no income effect, save
(possibly) such as is of a redistributive character. The quantities
of goods available, to consumers as a whole, are not greatly
altered; if this is so, we should not expect to find any great effect
upon our index-numbers, from these causes, either one way or
the other.

This is the general character of the effect, in such circumstances, of a major change in the relative prices of broad classes
of goods. But in addition to this change (which may well have a

perverse effect, though that will perhaps occur rather less commonly than might have appeared at first to be probable), there will inevitably be a multiplicity of minor changes in the price-ratios of commodities within the major groups. There is no reason why these should not have significant substitution effects that are small in themselves, but will contribute to the total substitution effect in a manner which in total is by no means negligible. This at least is what a closer examination would suggest to be likely, even in cases where a perverse effect on the index-numbers seems rather probable at first sight.

It would however be unwise to pursue such speculation farther. Our concern in this chapter has been with the refinement of a tool of analysis, not with its use. That this tool is capable of use is unquestionable; but the task of using it must be left to other hands.

XX

SUMMARY AND CONCLUSION

1. The prime concern of demand theory is with the law of demand. It is from the standpoint of its effect in elucidating and elaborating the law of demand that our theory may best be summarized, and that it may claim to be judged.

In its elementary form, the law of demand states no more than that the demand curve slopes downwards: that a fall in the price of a commodity tends to increase the quantity demanded, and that an increase in supply tends to lower price. Thus, even in its elementary form, the law has two aspects—price into quantity and quantity into price. At the elementary level, the two aspects do ordinarily appear as co-ordinate; but when the theory is elaborated, it has often happened that one aspect has been given some sort of primacy over the other. One of the things which we may claim to have done in this book is to have restored the balance between the two aspects—to have kept the theory facing both ways throughout.

In its elementary form, the theory only claims to be true 'other things being equal'; and the same qualification persists however far the process of generalization is carried. For generalization consists in nothing else but the letting of some 'other things' out of Marshall's 'pound'; but however many things we let out, some will always remain inside. There must always be causes, some of them no doubt most important causes, the operation of which cannot be studied by a theory of the present type. All that theory can do is to help in the isolation of these causes, in a particular case, by investigation of what would be likely to happen if such causes of change as we are not explicitly examining were out of operation.

It is for the purpose of this investigation, so defined, that we have to introduce a hypothesis; that which we have taken is the preference hypothesis, which seems to contain the essential part of the utility theory. We have taken some trouble to elaborate this hypothesis, especially from the point of view of seeing that we did not assume any more than was necessary for our particular purpose. It is desirable to do this, partly in order to make the applicability of the theory as wide as possible, partly because a careful choice of assumptions (as the logician would say, a correct selection of axioms) is bound to ease our further steps, especially in the later stages of the process of generalization.

It was for this reason, in the first place, that we rejected the 'cardinal' element in the utility function; we can do without it, and if it is not necessary, it is likely to be an encumbrance. It was also for this reason that we avoided assuming that the consumer has a complete scale of preferences, covering every conceivable alternative; all that we need is that he should be able to choose consistently (other things being equal) between such alternatives as are presented to his choice, or are closely similar to those presented to his choice. Finally, it was for the same reason that we interpreted the preference hypothesis in the sense of weak ordering—so that we avoided assuming the non-existence of alternatives between which the consumer is unable to choose. For weak ordering, as its name implies, is a weaker assumption than that of strong ordering; it avoids excluding a form of conduct (on the face of it, very natural and intelligible conduct) which the strong ordering assumption does exclude.

But, having gone so far, we found that we were in danger of going too far; if we assumed weak preference, and assumed no more than weak preference, we could not have a law of demand at all. In order to have a theory at all, the assumption of weak preference had to be filled out to some slight extent. Even when so filled out, it may still be claimed that the weak preference assumption is a minimal assumption; it is the least we have to assume in order to get a law of demand. Nevertheless it is an assumption which has some complexity of structure, and which is accordingly sufficient to support a good deal of development.

2. The first of the conclusions which we draw from the preference hypothesis (when finally formulated) are the consistency tests, being 'weak' forms of the tests of Revealed Preference to which Samuelson attaches such importance. Though it is admitted that these tests have an essential place in the structure of the theory, we have been unable to regard them (in Samuelson's manner) as significant direct tests of the preference hypothesis.

For the tests are essentially tests of individual behaviour; and the application of demand theory to individual behaviour does not appear to be a hopeful proceeding. The 'other things' which would have to remain equal, if individual behaviour is to satisfy consistency tests, are far more intricate and unmanageable than those which are likely to remain for consideration when we are concerned with the average (or aggregate) behaviour of large groups of individuals. The important thing which emerges at this stage is not the consistency tests, but the law of demand itself (though it may be fully admitted that the derivation of the law of demand from the consistency tests is the best way of establishing the law of demand). For the law of demand does apply, with full force, to the behaviour of groups as much as to the behaviour of individuals. This indeed is the characteristic which gives to that law its special importance.

Nevertheless, if we were only concerned with the law of demand in its elementary form, of a relation between the price and quantity demanded of a single commodity, the proceeding which we have adopted in order to establish it would be absurdly pretentious. For at this stage, all that this elaborate proceeding has added to the conclusions of common sense is a mere trifle: the elaboration of a rare exception (the Giffen case) which was already distinguished by Marshall, and which has more life in the minds of examinees than it could possibly have in the real world. But it has been a principal contention of this book that we do not need to stop there. A careful statement of the elementary theory, such as we have given in Parts I and II above, is useful, not for its own sake, but because of the further developments which can be based upon it. The theory of the demand for a single commodity is only the beginning of demand theory. The general theory of demand is a theory of the relation between the set of prices, at which purchases are made, and the set of quantities which are purchased. The foundations of demand theory have deserved careful definition, mainly because we are thereby enabled to get significant results in this wider field also.

3. It might well be supposed, at first sight, that the correct generalization of the law of demand, applied to a group of commodities the prices of which are changing in any manner, would be found by an expression of the elementary law in terms of

index-numbers. It would thus be maintained that (*ceteris paribus*) the quantity-index of the group and the price-index of the group would move in opposite directions. This is indeed what economists appear to assert, every time that they draw (for example) a demand curve for imports. But a simple example will serve to make it clear that there is unlikely to be any general *law* to this effect.

Consider two commodities X and Y, of which prices and quantities are initially such that their total money values are equal. Suppose that the price of X then rises by 10 per cent., while the price of Y falls by 20 per cent. The price-index of the group (on the initial position as base) would then have *fallen* from 100 (50+50) to 95 (55+40). Now suppose that there are no cross-effects, of the price of one on the demand for the other; suppose that the demand for X is highly elastic, while the demand for Y is highly inelastic; then there would be nothing extraordinary about a result in which the quantity demanded of X fell by 20 per cent., while that for Y remained nearly stationary. The quantity-index would then *fall* from 100 (50+50) to 90 (40+50). The price-index and the quantity-index would have moved in the same direction, although nothing at all had happened which common sense would regard as the least out of the way.

A 'law' which purported to say that things could not happen in this manner would be highly suspect. In order that there should be a tendency for the price and quantity indexes for a group to behave like the price and quantity of a single commodity, either the prices of the group, or the quantities of the group, must have some tendency to move together, so that the group is not too far from behaving like a single commodity. The true generalization of the law of demand is of quite a different character; it sets a much weaker restriction on what can happen.

If from one situation to another, there are several changes in prices, but there is no commodity of which the price and quantity move together in the same direction, the generalized law of demand (in its correct form) will be satisfied automatically; no restriction is set upon the size of the changes which can then take place. But there will now be no reason for surprise if there are some quantities that do move in the same direction as the corresponding prices; this can happen because of 'cross-effects' if for no other reason. The generalized law of demand does however set a limit on the extent to which such 'perverse' movements can occur. The sum-product of price-changes by quantity-changes (taken with proper attention to sign) must move in the same way as it would if only one price were changing. In this sense, the perverse movements must be swamped by the normal movements.

This generalized law is itself subject to a *ceteris paribus* clause, though it should be noted that since more things can vary, fewer things have to be held constant here than in the elementary theory. But as we extend the principle, the possibility of exceptions (even while other things remain equal) becomes more serious. The Giffen exception, which (as we have insisted) is in the elementary theory a matter of no importance, now sprouts into a series of exceptions, which are worthy of much more serious attention. For they are prototypes of the exceptions to which so many economic generalizations are subject; they have fellows, for instance, in the fields of welfare economics and of international trade theory, matters which lie altogether outside the scope of this book.

4. The generalized law of demand, when properly stated, is a symmetrical relation between price-changes and quantity-changes; it can accordingly be interpreted in a 'price into quantity' or in a 'quantity into price' manner, just as is the case with the elementary law. Thus we get the dualism between what we have called p-theory and q-theory; all the consequences of the law of demand (including the theory of substitutes and complements) can be developed either on p- or on q-lines. The results which emerge from the two approaches are sometimes the same (as when we get the same relation between the Laspeyre and Paasche price- and quantity-indexes), but they are sometimes notably different. Always, however, there is an exact parallelism between them. It should be of considerable convenience to know that we may walk either road, with due precaution, at our choice.

The distinction between p- and q-theory is particularly useful when it is applied to the topic of consumer's surplus. This is a field in which the corresponding concepts of the two types are closely similar to one another, but still distinguishable. It may indeed be maintained that it is only in those cases where the corresponding concepts differ to no more than a negligible extent that the whole method of consumer's surplus is of any use. But even so, it is desirable to know what happens when there is a divergence, for without this knowledge we can hardly tell when the method is usable and when not. But the results which can be got from using it, and the evaluation of those results, have not been our concern here. I hope to have more to say about them on another occasion, but I shall then approach them from a different, and a wider, point of view.

NOTE A

HARDLY had the first edition of this book been published, when I was besieged with letters from mathematical economists convicting me of a 'howler'. I had stated, on the top of p. 40, that 'a two-dimensional continuum cannot be strongly ordered'; and that, as I have now been fully convinced, is simply not true. Though the examples which were presented to me were sometimes recondite, I now appreciate that I ought to have been able to see the point for myself. For it is already apparent, on my 'striped' diagram (p. 41), that the stripes could have got indefinitely near together (so as to form a two-dimensional continuum); yet it would remain logically possible for a stripe which lay farther to the right to be preferable (as a whole) to any stripe which lay farther to the left, while within each stripe a higher point would be preferred to a lower.

It is logically possible, but not much more. For as I said, I could make no economic sense of this possibility, even when the stripes are to be separated by finite intervals; as the stripes get nearer together, the sense in the construction gets less and less. And the same seems to hold for other possibilities of the same sort. It is not necessary that the stripes should be vertical straight lines; they might take all sorts of shapes, but it would still have to be true that the consumer would reach a more preferred position by going along any stripe in a particular direction, and would *also* reach a more preferred position by going from *any* point on one stripe to *any* point on the next. I must now admit that these things are not ruled out by logic; but I must still hold that they are ruled out by a very elementary application of common sense.

There was another passage where I got into trouble with the same critics: my attempt to prove the existence of an indifferent position (pp. 70–71). But here I am more inclined to stand my ground. In order to prevent misunderstanding, I have substituted the word 'unbroken' for the 'continuous' which used to stand on line 25 of p. 71, and which (it is only too clear) served as a red rag to the mathematician. Otherwise I have left these pages unchanged. But I admit that this course needs justification, and I would offer the following as explanation of what I have done, or failed to do.

The case that is being considered is that in which there are two commodities that are objects of choice, X (which may only be available in discrete units) and M, or Money (which is finely divisible). It was explained on p. 40 what 'finely divisible' means. 'Though money is not finely divisible in the mathematical sense' (its quantity is not a continuous variable) 'the smallest monetary unit (farthing or cent) is so small in relation to the other units with which we are concerned that the imperfect divisibility of money is in practice a thing of no importance.' Thus, in application to the argument of p. 71, if we have shown (as we have shown) that, under the assumptions we are making, *either m* units of money are indifferent with so much X, *or* that so much X is preferred to m units of money, while $m+1$ units of money are preferred to it; in either case it is correct, within our field of discourse, to say that the given quantity of X is for our purposes indifferent with m (or $m+1$) units of money. Concretely, if the marginal valuation of a bicycle, or of a year's consumption of cabbages, lies between £20. 10s. $6\frac{1}{2}d.$ and £20. 10s. $6\frac{3}{4}d.$, it will do no harm if we reckon either price to *be* the marginal valuation; and it will do no serious harm if we round off and reckon the marginal valuation at £20. 10s. 6d., or even £20. 10s.

INDEX